REFLECTIONS
ON CREATING
LEARNING
ORGANIZATIONS

Other titles by Pegasus Communications, Inc.

The Systems Thinker™ newsletter
*Beyond Learning Organizations: Integrating Total Quality
Control and Systems Thinking*

The Toolbox Reprint Series
Systems Archetypes I
Systems Thinking Tools: A User's Reference Guide

REFLECTIONS
ON
CREATING
LEARNING
ORGANIZATIONS

EDITED BY KELLIE T. WARDMAN

Pegasus Communications, Inc.   Cambridge MA

Diagram from *Requisite Organization: The CEO's Guide to Creative Structure and Leadership* by Elliot Jaques. © 1989 Cason Hall & Co. Publishers, Falls Church, Virginia. Reprinted by permission.

Diagram from *Sloan Management Review*, "Leader's New Work" by Peter M. Senge. © 1990 Sloan Management Review Association, Cambridge, Massachusetts. Reprinted by permission.

Quotation from *Leadership and the New Science* © 1992 by Margaret J. Wheatley. Berrett-Koehler Publishers, San Francisco, California. Reprinted by permission.

Front cover photograph, Yosemite National Park, California © Michael Goodman.

Reflections on Creating Learning Organizations. Copyright © 1994 by Pegasus Communications, Inc.
First Printing June 1994

Pegasus Communications, Inc. is dedicated to helping organizations soar to new heights of excellence. By providing the forum and resources, Pegasus helps managers explore, understand, and articulate the challenges they face in managing the complexities of a changing business world. For information about *The Systems Thinker*™ newsletter, the annual **Systems Thinking in Action Conference**, volume discounts, or other publications, contact Pegasus Communications, Inc., PO Box 120 Kendall Square, Cambridge, MA 02142-0001 USA. Phone (617) 576-1231, Fax (617) 576-3114.

 Printed on recycled paper (50% recycled waste, including 10% post-consumer waste).

ISBN 1-883823-03-X

 Pegasus Communications, Inc.
PO Box 120 Kendall Square
Cambridge, MA 02142-0001
(617) 576-1231, fax (617) 576-3114

Dedicated to all of the practitioners
who are sustaining the vision
and working to create learning organizations.

ACKNOWLEDGMENTS

I would like to thank all of the authors who contributed to *Reflections on Creating Learning Organizations* for their dedication and work in the field. In addition, thanks to Colleen Lannon-Kim for extensive editorial support on the original articles, and much appreciation to Michelle Minoff for the book and cover design and to Michael R. Goodman for the cover photograph.

CONTENTS

BEGINNING THE JOURNEY

The journey of creating a learning organization begins on the *inside*. It begins with a commitment among individuals in an organization to reexamine their ways of thinking about the world. And it necessitates a shift from the traditional external focus on the environment, the economy, and competition, to an internal focus on the organizational systems and structures that inhibit the results we want.

Much of the work that has evolved in organizational development over the years is consistent with the visions of a learning organization. Since the first organizations were developed, people have been talking about how to improve work relationships, processes, and results. But systems thinking and its related disciplines are not just about improving organizational relationships—they are about fundamentally enhancing an organization's capacity to create its own future. A learning organization must therefore be committed to viewing its organizational structures systemically. In addition, it must be dedicated to using the tools of systems thinking to create a healthy community where its members are free to explore new ways of working and thinking.

Creating learning organizations requires *giving up* our never-ending search for the great panacea. Instead, the focus is on the long-term structural change that will produce sustainable results. Creating this change will be rewarding—but it can be difficult and perhaps painful. Many organizations may not yet be prepared to reexamine their historical ways of operating. Many people may not be willing to challenge their assumptions or to admit they even have them. To become learning organizations, however, we must first be willing to surface and question our comfortable mental models of how "the world is."

Many managers are now beginning to realize that it is time to make dramatic changes in the way we operate. People who care deeply about making such changes and are committed to creating the capacities of a learning organization have been working toward that end for many years. A small number of these individuals are included as contributing authors in *Reflections on Creating Learning Organizations*. Their work is intended to be a catalyst for your own thinking about organizations. The articles do not necessarily need to be read in order—each one is centered around a particular theme and therefore stands on its own. There is, however, a natural progression through the articles, and you may find it most beneficial to read them in the order they are presented.

The first two articles, "If People Are Assets, Why Do We Treat Them Like Expenses" (p. 19) and "Double-Loop Accounting: A Language for the Learning Organization" (p. 27) challenge the most fundamental assumptions about our organizational processes—those around our methods for tracking and measuring financial health and assets. Both articles beg the question "Are there better ways to structure information flows to support the creation of a learning organization?" These articles expose the assumptions behind our current systems and explore new ways of thinking that can help an organization to manage its own development.

"Systemic Quality Management: Improving the Quality of Doing and Thinking" (p. 35) begins to move from an operational focus to a conceptual one. This article discusses a new management paradigm that blends the operational focus of Total Quality with the conceptual strength of systems thinking. "Managing Organizational Learning Cycles" (p. 43) continues the theme of operational and conceptual learning by presenting a model for how organizations can capture individual learning. Mental models, or views of the world, are described in this article as the critical pathway between individual and organizational learning.

"Paradigm-Creating Loops: How Perceptions Shape Reality" (p. 53) discusses the traditional problem-solving model of managing—and explains why creating learning organizations requires rethinking how we articulate and address problems. The "Ladder of Inference," a tool developed by Chris Argyris, helps provide a framework for exploring the mental models that both define and complicate our organizational problems. "Unlocking Organizational Routines that Prevent Learning" (p. 61) continues this discussion by describing some case examples in which organizational defensive routines hamper learning. In addition, this article conveys the strength and usefulness of action maps, a tool that can be used to reduce defensive routines.

"Human Dynamics: A Foundation for the Learning Organization" (p. 71) begins to discuss how fundamental distinctions in the way people function can affect the way we think, learn, and work together. Beginning to understand the different personality dynamics offered by this model can help provide a foundation of human understanding and development that can enhance conversations and teamwork.

"Dialogue: The Power of Collective Thinking" (p. 83) discusses the practice and challenges of dialogue, an approach to collective conversation and shared thinking that enables entirely new levels of creativity to emerge. The levels and stages of dialogue described in this article help provide a framework within which teams can begin to understand what real dialogue requires and how it can allow entirely new kinds of collective intelligence to appear. "The Emergence of Learning Communities" (p. 95) probes further into creating spaces for learning in organizations, by describing the stages of community development. This piece also delves into the structure of collaborative learning and attempts to diagram the structure behind limits to learning.

Finally, "The Spirit of the Learning Organization" (p. 107) begins to address key challenges for the learning organization—how to develop a commitment to the truth (an organization's shared values) and a commitment to multiple truths in the support of diversity of opinions and ideas. It explores the questions about the role of leaders in these organizations and contains a beginning list of values for a learning organization. And "How Do You Know if Your Organization is Learning?"

(p. 115) attempts to address the challenge of measuring learning and begins to describe what a learning organization might look and feel like.

These articles represent just the beginning—the beginning of an entirely new way of thinking and working. There are no clear answers or defined pathways for this journey, but there are many ideas to guide us along the way and tools that will help us to manage more effectively and think more systemically. And as we begin to work toward creating what we know is possible, we can begin to let go of the need to have a perfectly clear picture of what a learning organization will look like. But in the process, we can be assured that we will be practicing the belief that *the most effective way to cope with change is to help create it.*

To help you in this exciting journey, here are some reflections on creating learning organizations.

—Kellie T. Wardman
Editor

I, too, can feel the ground shaking.
I hear its deep rumblings.
Any moment now, the earth will crack open
and I will stare into its dark center.
Into that smoking caldera,
I will throw most of what I have treasured,
most of the techniques and tools
that have made me feel competent.
I cannot do that yet;
I cannot just heave everything
I know into the abyss.
But I know it is coming. And when it comes,
when I have made my sacrificial offerings
to the gods of understanding, then the ruptures will cease.
Healing waters will cover the land,
giving birth to new life,
burying forever the ancient,
rusting machines of our past understandings.
And on these waters I will set sail to places
I only now imagine.
There I will be blessed with new visions and new magic.

—Margaret J. Wheatley
Leadership and the New Science

If People Are Assets, Why Do We Treat Them Like Expenses?

by Daniel H. Kim

There is a lot of talk in the business community about "people being our most important assets." It sounds like a good idea—recognizing people as valuable assets as opposed to line-item expenses. But has the idea been translated into fundamentally new actions and policies? A quick glance through the financial statements of any organization reveals that, when it comes to the bottom line, we have not changed our thinking about people as expenses. "People" only show up as a cost of sales, a selling expense, or an R&D expense. On the balance sheet, they appear as payroll liabilities.

If people really are a company's most important asset, it is strange that most companies do so little to keep track of, understand, and benefit from their full capabilities. Aside from payroll costs, number of employees, and headcount by department or function, there is little information available for assessing the intellectual capital of an organization. Yet there is an abundance of *usable* information for managing capital equipment, inventories, and other physical (or financial) assets.

If financial statements were merely used as snapshots for reporting an organization's status to its stockholders, this omission would not be a problem. Unfortunately, financial accounting data is also used for *managing* the business (see "Double-Loop Accounting: A Language for the Learning Organization, p. 27). As long as we manage our organizations according to current financial accounting measures, people are likely to be treated as variable costs and nothing more.

REDEFINING "ASSETS"

If you were to ask a coach or conductor about the capacity of a team or orchestra, he or she would be able to tell you in great detail about the capability of each individual. Their job is to understand and build upon those individual capabilities to enhance the capacity of the whole group. They create synergy by making the whole performance more than the sum of the individual parts.

A lot of good managers see their job as precisely that of coach and mentor. They understand the organizational needs and recognize the importance of developing people who can meet and exceed those needs. But how does that normally get translated into an organization's financial statement? The people who are "appreciating" are given promotions and raises that show up on financial statements as higher expenses—without a concomitant visible increase in the asset base of the company. As employees grow more productive, they show up as higher expenses. When times are good, the higher expenses are "covered." But when times get bad, people tend to be seen as expenses that can be cut.

A football team does not lay off half of its starting players because it had a bad season and revenues were down. To try to go through a season with half as many players is not going to improve its chances of winning. Of course, it is a lot clearer what capabilities are necessary to create a winning football team than those of a successful company. In the absence of such clarity, we hire and fire people as if only the total *number* of people is important and not their *capabilities*.

What if we *really* treated employees as assets—not just in words but on our financial statements? For starters, we would add another category in the asset column and devise a way to assess the value of the intellectual capital of the organization. Unlike physical assets, people assets could *appreciate* over time. We would still account for people's salaries, benefits, and other employee-related costs as expenses, but we would also have a corresponding valuation for the people-capacity of the organization. The people-asset column would provide corporate visibility that the people-capacity was being enhanced.

Putting employees on the balance sheet as assets could also change the way we think about cost-cutting. Training would be viewed as an investment and would not be automatically cut when times get tough. Vacation days would be considered vital investments that help our most important assets become even more productive. Employees would not be seen as expenses to be cut out, but assets in which we could invest and expect to get a return in terms of higher productivity, new products, better quality, and a myriad of other possibilities that we have not yet begun to identify.

THE LEARNING ORGANIZATION'S DILEMMA

Being able to track the appreciating value of people-assets could help address a dilemma that arises out of continual learning and improvement in worker productivity. A vice president of quality at a semiconductor manufacturer posed the dilemma this way: *If a company is pursuing quality improvement and the productivity of the workforce is continuously improving, either the company has to keep growing at the same rate or it has to continually reduce its workforce.*

His experience told him that an annual improvement of 20 percent was reasonable and sustainable over a long period of time. But if the company improves productivity by 20 percent (that is, the same number of people can produce 20 percent more than before), what should they do with the additional people that are freed up? He argued that the only options were to keep growing the company (by expanding current business or redeploying the people into new markets) or to lay off the workers (and distribute the additional profits to the stockholders). When his own company was unable to expand during a drawn-out industry slump, people were laid off. The message to the employees was that they were improving themselves out of a job. Improvement rates slowed considerably.

A learning organization faces a similar problem as it learns to become more effective on all fronts. The annual rate of improvement can be substantially higher than 20 percent, which may make the pain of the productivity growth even more acute. What happens as people "learn" themselves out of their current jobs? If they are redeployed into new markets, continually expanding the company, the organization could either hit diminishing returns as it expands and loses focus, or it might have to lay off its workers. Neither alternative is very attractive.

A MODEST PROPOSAL

One possible solution to this dilemma is to allow companies with appreciating people-assets to contribute those employees who wish to take on a new challenge to a non-profit organization for a period of time and take a tax deduction for it.

By allowing companies to redeploy their people-assets outside of the firm, a number of problems can be addressed. First, it gives companies an option other than endless expansion or layoffs. It can also provide employees with tremendous opportunities which they normally would have to leave the company to pursue. Second, it helps address non-profit companies' need for technical expertise and experienced professional managers. Matching the asset of a knowledgeable worker with the needs of a nonprofit can be far more valuable than any monetary contributions. Third, corporations can become more directly involved in the role of distributor of wealth within their local communities. Corporations have always been wealth creators as well as wealth distributors, but the emphasis has been more on creation. Distribution of wealth has primarily come in the form of employment, dividend payments, and charitable donations.

Allowing tax deductions for such actions begins to blur the artificial distinction between for-profit and non-profit organizations. Both types of organizations are responsible for producing the maximum return to their stakeholders. From a systemic perspective, however, the distinction is artificial in the sense that we are all stakeholders to varying degrees in both types of enterprises.

Stratum	Time-span	Level of Task Complexity	People Capacity Required
VII	50Y	Strategic options: alternative routes to make or transform operating systems	Set long-term operational perspective/culture/values
VI	20Y	Whole wide-world data accumulation and diagnosis	Gear corporate mission/culture/values with BU mission and development
V	10Y	Practical judgment of immediate & downstream consequences of changes	Policy leadership and direction of BU
IV	5Y	Parallel processing and trading off	Set climate for MRU's
III	2Y	Construct alternative routes to goals	Mutual recognition leadership
II	1Y	Data accumulation and diagnosis	Direct face-to-face leadership
I	3M / 1D	Direct judgment	Face-to-face, day-to-day peer groups

Source: Jaques, 1989

How should the belief that employees are a company's most important asset be translated into visible actions? How can an organization actually operationalize that value into something that can make a strategic difference? To address these questions, we need a framework for identifying what "people-capacity" is and how that capacity can support the needs of the organization.

One possibility can be found in the book *Requisite Organization* by Elliott Jaques (Cason Hall, 1989). Jaques proposes that the work of *any* organization falls into eight different strata, each corresponding to a specific time-span. For the learning organization, the eight levels can serve as broad categories in which one would want to develop their people-assets. Internal measures could be developed to see how well one is progressing on developing people's effectiveness within each stratum. Jaques even proposes an equation for evaluating people's "working capacity" as a function of cognitive power, skills, and task type.

The nature of the work, as defined by the time-span measure, could determine the compensation as well as the fit of a person to fill that position. A person who is capable of constructing alternative routes to goals (level 3), for example, may have great difficulty moving into level 4, which requires parallel processing and trading off among alternatives. When the actual working capacity in any of the strata exceeds the required working capacity, some people can be redeployed either within the organization or outside the organization (perhaps to nonprofit companies).

Think Globally, Act Locally

Implementing this proposal could radically change the role of both business and government in community development (see "Direct Channel to the Community"). Currently, the U.S. federal government serves as the largest centralized institution for redeploying wealth back into the community. The bureaucracy required to run such a system rivals the now-dismantled system of the former Soviet Union. The federal government's role could shift toward providing the laws, incentives, guidelines, and information to work toward the common good. The people and organizations closest to the local conditions could have the freedom to act in their local interest—thinking globally, acting locally.

As the role of business becomes redefined as an active community player, perhaps a new corporate measure will become a standard by which a company will be assessed by society—its non-profit-to-profit (N/P) ratio. The ratio could serve as an indicator of how effectively an organization can develop its people-assets to create a surplus that would

DIRECT CHANNEL TO THE COMMUNITY

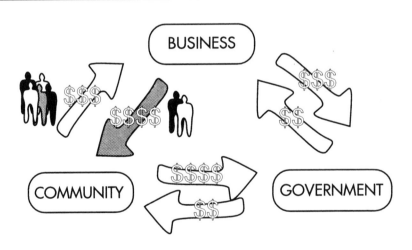

The ability to take "people-deductions" allows companies to deploy some of their workforce directly into the community. This short-circuits the usual flow of money: from companies through the government (social services, research funds, and grants), and—after much delay and many dollars chewed up in the process—to the community.

then support the work of non-profits and social programs. The higher the ratio, the more effective the organization is in producing returns to society.

By giving a tax deduction for redeploying employees in non-profits, much of the means and responsibility for community development and social work can be turned over to those who are local citizens (individuals and corporations). It will not only redefine the role of government, but also the purpose of business.

The scope and scale of change implicated by such a shift is enormous and would require a long time horizon. But the current system is in need of a serious overhaul. The Social Security system is basically bankrupt. Poverty and homelessness are on the rise. Bureaucratic inefficiencies continue to chew up millions of dollars (as well as people). Our education system is in a state of crisis and lags far behind that of most industrialized countries.

As professor John Sterman of the MIT Sloan School of Management pointed out in *The Systems Thinker* ("Not All Recessions Are Created Equal," February 1991), the downturn of the economic long wave "is a time of radical change." The imbalances it generates spill out into the social and political realm, creating new threats and opportunities— in effect, changing the rules of the game. Just as the seeds of the growth of the federal government were sown at the last trough of the long wave, perhaps a new direction can be plotted as we near the bottom of the current cycle.

Daniel H. Kim is the publisher of The Systems Thinker™ *and director of the Learning Lab Research Project at the MIT Organizational Learning Center.*

Double-Loop Accounting: A Language for the Learning Organization

by Fred Kofman

I f accountants ("those bean-counters") are so dumb and we ("who really know this business") are so smart, why do they run our companies? We complain that budget-mania closes off profitable ventures. We blame accountants when we scramble to meet performance goals. "It's not our fault," we say. "We have no choice but to wreak havoc on our company's long-term well-being; we must manage by the numbers. The enemy is *out there*." Or is it?

There has been much grumbling in recent years about the outdated accounting systems that are straitjacketing most companies. Some innovators have implemented new systems—activity-based accounting, non-financial performance measures, critical success factor analysis. But most reforms fall short because their underlying purpose remains the same—to provide financial control by "keeping score" in the game of business. This is like coaching a team by looking at the points on the scoreboard rather than by watching the action on the field. If we want our accounting systems to foster a learning organization, their primary purpose should change radically. Instead of describing what already happened, they must enhance a group's ability to explore, articulate and understand their reality.

The Language of Business
Accounting has long been called the "language of business." Most of us

think of language as a means for describing the world around us, just as accounting describes the status of an organization. But the power of language goes much further. It can serve as a medium through which we create new understandings and new realities as we begin to talk about them. In fact, we don't talk about what we see; *we see only what we can talk about.*

Our perspectives on the world depend on the interaction of our nervous system and our language—both act as filters through which we perceive our world. In business terms, the language and information systems of an organization are not an objective means of describing an outside reality—they fundamentally structure the perceptions and actions of its members. To reshape the measurement and communication systems of a company is to reshape all potential interactions at the most fundamental level. Language (accounting) as articulation of reality is more primordial than strategy, structure, or corporate culture.

Management accounting systems both communicate and shape the goals of an organization. They form the communication channels that enable a decentralized enterprise to run as a coherent body. When they confront individuals with the global consequences of their actions, they can unite the organization toward a common goal. When they promote sub-optimization and defensive routines, they can blind the organization to the point of disintegration.

If accounting systems are to support the activities of the learning organization, we need to recognize that these systems are very much tied into our mental models—they dictate where our attention should be focused. In most organizations we don't measure what is important, we measure what is measurable. How do we know, then, if organizational learning is occurring if we can't measure it?

DOUBLE-LOOP ACCOUNTING— GOING "META"

The concept of double-loop accounting is the analog of Chris Argyris and Donald Schön's work on single-loop and double-loop learning. In

How did we get into this mess?
(Or, the history of accounting)

How did control become interpreted as manipulation instead of detection and correction of error? How did accounting turn into scorekeeping instead of strategy-supporting? Why didn't we think of accounting as a neural-linguistic system that enables a group to coordinate its perceptions, interpretations, and actions in pursuit of a common goal? A historical reconstruction of the origins of accounting is both an answer to these questions and a first step toward changing the future.

In the Middle Ages, as overseas trade flourished, merchants began banding together and collectively buying ships to transport their goods. Because of the high-risk investment required, groups of traders pooled their resources to spread the risk. (This is the same idea behind the stock market: spread the risk so shareholders can maintain low-risk portfolios even if their shares are invested in high-risk companies.)

Although the merchants owned the ship, the captain was solely responsible for managing their investment. The merchants needed some guarantees that their money would be spent wisely. They developed a series of control measures that have evolved into our complex system of modern financial accounting—the way companies communicate with their stakeholders through financial statements, earnings forecasts, quarterly reports, etc.

By the 19th century, the industrial revolution was pushing companies to grow larger and larger. Economies of scale and scope fostered organizations whose size exceeded the management capacity of existing methods. Managerial accounting systems, which allow companies to communicate internally, became neces-sary. These systems were intended to give the managers a yardstick for evaluating their performance, pinpoint problem areas or future possibilities, and communicate the status of their department to others. Though the purpose was different from financial accounting systems, they borrowed many of the same policies and practices.

Financial accounting systems are designed for stewardship, control, and external reporting. They are focused on gathering accurate information—providing snapshots of the business. Managerial accounting, however, is about understanding the dynamics of the business and how today's actions impact the future. Both accounting systems are necessary for a productive economy. The problem is that we are using financial reports to inform our management.

Financial accountants are sort of like insurance company doctors—their job is to make sure that the company is not misrepresenting its "health" to those who pay the bills. They are ultimately concerned with costs. There is nothing wrong with insurance company doctors—there wouldn't be health insurance without them—but we wouldn't go to them for treatment. The relationship of openness and trust we develop with our personal physicians is vital for effective treatment. Similarly, there is nothing wrong with financial accountants—there wouldn't be publicly-held companies without them—but we shouldn't let them run our companies. By putting financial accountants in charge of creating and maintaining managerial accounting systems, in effect we are letting our companies be run by the insurance company's doctor.

single-loop learning, people respond to changes in their organizational environment by detecting errors and correcting them to maintain the current or desired status. Single-loop learning does not encourage any reflection or inquiry that may lead to a reframing of the situation—it focuses on analyzing and correcting the problem at hand. Double-loop learning, in contrast, involves surfacing and challenging deep-rooted assumptions and norms of an organization that may lead to a reformulation of the problem.

Similarly, while single-loop accounting explains *how* things are being done, double-loop accounting explores *why* they are done that way. If we used single-loop accounting to evaluate a quality improvement program in our company, we would first set a goal (such as a 50 percent reduction in defects) and develop strategies for reaching that goal—training programs, more quality inspections, and dismissal threats for workers with high numbers of defects. We would then gather data to gauge our improvement (such as number of defects per 1000 parts), evaluate our progress, and implement corrective actions (see "Double-Loop Accounting").

Say at the end of the first year we get a report that says quality only increased 20 percent. A typical single-loop response might be, "It seems our workers still aren't committed to quality. Our initial training programs didn't go far enough. Let's raise their awareness with slogans to educate them and fire some more people to show we're serious."

With double-loop accounting we would go through a similar strategy development, data collection, and evaluation process, but our analysis would go one step further. Rather than only questioning what was wrong with our implementation strategy, we would begin to question how our policies and structures might actually be impeding the employees' quality efforts. We would begin to explore the governing structures of the organization that are behind the outcomes.

For example, say we took a tour of the shop floor and noticed "Quality is #1" signs posted everywhere. We talked with the workers and heard their frustration about taking blame for quality problems beyond their control. Talking further we learned that their individual bonuses depend on how many chips they produce above or below the plant's average. We might begin to hypothesize that the problem is not with the workers' commitment to quality, but with the division's management philosophy.

Double-loop accounting prompts us to "go meta"—to get below the surface and explore the philosophy underlying the unsuccessful actions. What leads the managers to believe that workers are not committed? How can they inquire into the workers' claims of frustrating conditions? How can we synthesize managers' and workers' understandings (and misunderstandings) into a coherent picture that they can use to take effective action? In essence, double-loop accounting takes us beyond the simple reporting of numbers. It questions where those num-

DOUBLE-LOOP ACCOUNTING

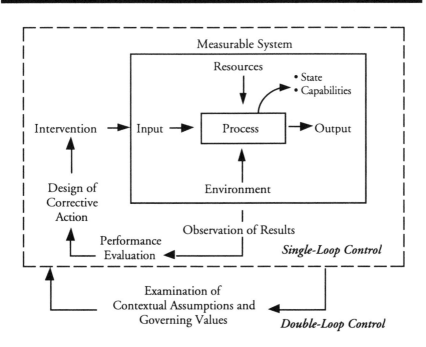

Single-loop accounting focuses on analyzing and correcting the problem at hand (top). Double-loop accounting prompts us to get below the surface and explore the underlying perceptions and values that are behind the outcomes.

bers came from, why they are important, and allows us to pinpoint leverage points for creating effective change.

DOUBLE-LOOP ACCOUNTING IN PRACTICE

I have had the opportunity to participate in efforts to revamp the management accounting systems of two major automobile companies. These companies started general overhauls of their cost systems to gain a more accurate picture of actual costs. However, in their fascination with technological solutions, they placed little attention on creating levers for translating these reports into effective actions. The new activity-based costing system gave them a more accurate picture of current reality (single-loop accounting), but it did not help them to explore ways of articulating a common understanding and improve the system as a whole (double-loop accounting).

About a year ago, a plant manager, a department head, and I began an experiment at an engine plant: we designed and implemented a new performance management system based on double-loop accounting principles. In essence, we expanded the concerns of the measurement system to three areas: observation, common interpretation, and coordinated action. Instead of imposing a new reporting system from our "expert" perspective, we started by asking the workers what would help them better understand their impact on the department's performance.

We helped workers design and produce "Daily Performance Reports." These reports gave them immediate feedback on the performance of the department—quality levels, scrap rates, tooling costs—in terms that they could understand. When they experimented with different procedures, they were able to see immediately how those procedures contributed to the productivity of the department. Although the "Daily Performance Reports" might be considered inaccurate from a general accounting perspective, they helped the employees gain ownership of the numbers and improve their systemic understanding of how their actions contribute to the plant's performance. The project is now being extended to several other departments in the engine plant.

Corporate Umpires

Three baseball umpires were discussing their views on balls and strikes. "I call 'em as I see 'em," said the first, a realist. "I see 'em as I call 'em," said the second, an idealist. "They ain't nothin' 'til I call 'em," said the third, an existentialist. Depending on which view we take, we probably see accountants as bean-counters, business controllers, or cultural architects.

Umpires and rules do a lot more than define strikes and balls, they allow the game itself to exist. Likewise, accounting and accountants do a lot more than define profitable divisions and products, they allow capitalism itself to exist in its present form. "Infield fly" rules determine strategy, game outcomes, and player contracts; profitability rules determine promotions, plant closings and workers' lives.

I see the task of management accounting as the design of a *corporate nervous system*, a system tailored to structure an informational environment where the organization can position itself for maximum strength and flexibility. A "good" accounting system should allow managers to interpret a complex reality in ways that open fruitful possibilities for action. It should lead managers to ask the right questions—as opposed to provide them with the wrong answers.

If we understand how the information and incentive mechanisms of an organization condition its ability to learn, we can begin to design new systems that nourish (instead of strangle) creativity and innovation. Rather than being impediments to innovation, accounting systems could become the very drivers toward the development of a learning organization.

Fred Kofman is a professor at the MIT Sloan School of Management. He is directing one of the pilot projects of the MIT Organizational Learning Center, which explores ways to better coordinate the operations of a decentralized supply chain.

Systemic Quality Management: Improving the Quality of Doing and Thinking

by Daniel H. Kim

"No matter how hard Western nations try to engage in Quality Control education, they may not catch up with Japan until the 1990s, since it requires ten years for the QC education to take effect," quality expert Dr. Joseph Juran warned in 1981. Ten years later, Juran's prediction seems overly optimistic. Japanese companies passed the West in the quality marathon sometime in the 1980s, and they show no sign of slowing down.

Juran's message is all the more ominous if we consider Analog Devices president Ray Stata's theory. He believes that, contrary to the Boston Consulting Group's learning curve theory, "learning, properly managed, occurs as a function of time, independent of cumulative volume." The implication of his statement is startling: *we will never catch up with the Japanese because they have a permanent head start on us.* In other words, we can't expect to win the quality race by simply imitating the Japanese; we must innovate and improve upon Total Quality Control.

Integrating TQC and systems thinking can accelerate organizational learning beyond the current capabilities of TQC methods. The two approaches form a synergistic pair whose individual strengths complement each other and provide a balance of learning at all levels of an organization. Used together, they can help build a shared understanding of both conceptual insights and operational processes, forming a powerful new management paradigm I call Systemic Quality Management (SQM).

Beyond TQC: Systemic Quality Management

To be lasting and significant, organizational learning must advance on both the *operational* and *conceptual* levels. Operational learning means improving behaviors or ways of doing things—changing a machine setting, for example—in order to enhance the performance of a particular system. Conceptual learning involves changing one's mental models about how the world works, such as reframing a problem in a different context and exploring the implications. Learning at one level without the other is like trying to run a race with one foot nailed to the starting line—you may get off to a quick start, but you won't go very far.

The Systemic Quality Management (SQM) model combines systems thinking, with its conceptual basis, and TQC, with its operational emphasis, into an integrated management paradigm (see "SQM Model"). The top dashed box of the SQM model represents the traditional system dynamics problem-solving approach of gathering data, articulating the issues involved, building a model, running simulation analyses, identifying leverage points, and proposing policy changes. An implicit assumption of this process is that the insights generated will be compelling enough to produce action. In reality, however, policy change recommendations are not always implemented due to a lack of strong operational methods such as those TQC provides.

The bottom dashed box shows a typical TQC quality improvement process—the PDCA (Plan-Do-Check-Act) cycle. Requests from upper management are translated into a plan of action and checkpoints are determined for monitoring progress. The plans are then incorporated into the budget cycle and implemented. Any deviations found at the checkpoints are analyzed, and actions are taken to correct any discrepancies. Although the PDCA cycle works very well in implementing strategic plans and maintaining control over current processes, it is relatively weak where systems thinking is most helpful—identifying the high-leverage areas that drive the whole process.

Systemic Quality Management blends the conceptual strength of systems thinking and the operational focus of Total Quality into a seamless process. In a manufacturing environment, for example, the PDCA process could help line workers gather data, plot and analyze them, and determine how to make improvements to reduce equipment downtime and increase on-time delivery performance. A systemic study may reveal, however, that the timing of marketing efforts and production schedules systematically produces demand/supply imbalances, creating periods of deteriorating delivery performance (see "Marketing-Production

SQM MODEL

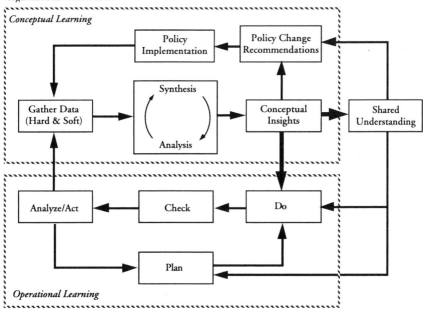

Traditional model of system dynamics organizational intervention

Conceptual Learning

Policy Implementation

Policy Change Recommendations

Synthesis

Gather Data (Hard & Soft)

Analysis

Conceptual Insights

Shared Understanding

Analyze/Act

Check

Do

Plan

Operational Learning

TQC's PDCA cycle

The Systemic Quality Management (SQM) model fuses the conceptual strength of systems thinking (top) and the operational focus of Total Quality methods (bottom) into a seamless process.

Connection"). The real leverage may lie in coordinating the activities of the two functions by building a shared understanding of how the two are interdependent.

The Systemic Quality Management model emphasizes the importance of creating shared understanding about the whole system. Building shared understanding through the use of systems thinking tools such as management flight simulators and learning labs can enhance the *PLAN*ning and *DO*ing steps of the PDCA cycle by providing a common base of conceptual models. The analysis and action produced through the PDCA cycle can, in turn, generate new data which would feed into the data gathering process and the next cycle of the *PLAN*ning stage. By fusing these two methodologies, Systemic Quality Management provides an integrated and balanced approach to organizational learning.

MARKETING/PRODUCTION CONNECTION

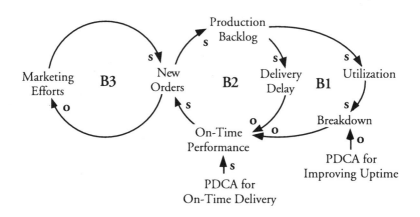

A successful marketing campaign produces a bulge in orders, swamping the factory. The factory starts to run at maximum capacity to get the orders out the door, but on-time performance suffers (B1). New orders fall as customers experience long delays (B2). As new orders slow down, the factory is able to improve on its delivery performance. But in the meantime, marketing has decided to launch a new campaign to counter the fall in new orders (B3), starting the cycle again.

TQC as a Vehicle for Organizational Learning

TQC's contribution to organizational learning is strongest on the operational side. But TQC is not just about improving production steps and reducing cycle times—it is a *thought revolution in management.* TQC has forced managers to abandon old mental models of viewing quality/cost and quality/productivity as either/or decisions. It is also changing managers' definition of quality from conforming to specifications to satisfying customers' needs.

The concept of building-in quality rather than inspecting-in quality has prompted a major shift in the way managers once viewed the production process. This change in the prevailing mental model has driven solid achievements at the operational level: Statistical Quality Control (SQC) has improved quality and lowered production costs through smaller variances and reduced scrap rates; separate quality inspectors are becoming obsolete as workers learn to inspect their own work for defects; and a customer-oriented approach has increased customer satisfaction.

As quality steadily improves at companies using TQC, there is no doubt that a great deal of learning continues to take place at the operational level. But beyond the initial mental breakthrough required at the outset of instituting TQC, new learning opportunities at the conceptual level become less available. Managers can go on advocating improvements *within* the current framework of organizational policies and traditions without gaining much insight about the whole system.

Systems Thinking and Organizational Learning

Unlike TQC's more operational focus, systems thinking's underpinnings are conceptual in nature. Systems thinking advocates approaching problems from the basis of the whole, rather than reducing problems to individual pieces and trying to understand each part. Whereas TQC focuses on *analyzing* the separate parts that make up the whole, systems thinking strives to *synthesize* the constituent parts.

Systems thinking helps break through functional walls in organizations by providing a framework for understanding the importance of managing the interconnections between various functions. Systems thinking is also useful for gaining deeper insights into the nature of complex systems, finding leverage points within the system, and testing assumptions about the viability of various policies.

By emphasizing the importance of trying to *understand* a problem, not simply *solve* it, systems thinking attempts to transform problem-solving organizations into *learning organizations.* A learning organization is one that consciously manages its learning processes through an inquiry-driven orientation among all its members. That is, learning organizations *actively and explicitly* encourage both operational and conceptual learning to ensure that areas of strategic importance are not neglected.

Building a learning organization means continually developing the capacity to create one's vision of the future. In order to design and implement effective policies and achieve desired results, managers need to look at their organization and its environment as a unified system. A systems perspective makes it easier to pinpoint the high-leverage actions that will produce significant, long-lasting improvements. But acquiring such an understanding will require ongoing management education that trains managers to blend analysis and synthesis into a new style of thinking. As they do, managers will begin to take on new roles and acquire new skills.

RESEARCHER AND THEORY-BUILDER

In learning organizations, managers are responsible for enhancing the quality of their *thinking*, not just the quality of their *doing*. This means becoming theory-builders: creating new frameworks for continually testing strategies, policies, and decisions. It also requires the skills and inquiring perspective of a researcher who is engaged in active experimentation. Unfortunately, we usually think of experimentation in organizations as "Hey, I'm just trying something new so don't hold me accountable," or "Let's see what happens." In such a setting, there is little opportunity for learning. Real experimentation means that managers, as researchers and theory-builders, actively formulate hypotheses and conduct "controlled" experiments to test them. Systems thinking provides an array of tools for running such experiments. Two in particular are management flight simulators and learning laboratories.

CREATING LEARNING ENVIRONMENTS

The necessary elements for learning are a set of tools, a context for the learning, and a structured setting for conducting experiments. Baseball teams, for example, have their equipment, game rules, and practice fields. Airline pilots have flight simulators, air space grids, and simulated flight conditions. No team would dream of starting the regular season without practice games, nor would airlines risk multi-million dollar airplanes and the lives of hundreds of passengers in order for pilots to learn by trial-and-error.

Managers, on the other hand, do not have comparable tools and environments for experimenting and learning—in management, initiation by fire is the rule. However, management flight simulators now offer managers the equivalent of a pilot's flight simulator, so they can experiment with various policies without fear of "crashing and burning" real companies.

Appropriately, the first management flight simulator developed at the MIT Sloan School of Management was based on an airline—People Express. Each entering class of masters students at the Sloan School spends a day developing their strategy and "piloting" the simulated airline (see "'Flying' People Express Again," *The Systems Thinker,* November 1990 for a more complete description of the simulator). Each team makes five quarterly decisions as the players struggle to manage the growth of the start-up airline. Spreadsheets, graphs, and internal management reports containing competitor and market information help them chart their progress. Through repeated trial-and-error experimentation, the students gain simulated experience facing the challenges of managing a rapid-growth company. People Express and other simulators are currently in wide use in academia as well as corporations.

If the simulator is analogous to a sports team's equipment, the learning lab can be thought of as a manager's practice field. Learning labs provide a structured learning environment where management teams can test out new strategies and policies, reflect on the outcomes, and collectively discuss the central issues. Managers can accelerate time by rapidly simulating a real life system and then stopping the flow of time at each decision point to reflect on their actions.

By making operating assumptions explicit and testing those assumptions within the learning lab, managers are encouraged to reflect not only on the quality of their decisions, but on how they arrived at those decisions. The learning lab environment promotes conceptual learning by helping managers develop an inquiry mode of learning—to continually "think about their thinking" and break away from outmoded frames and perceptions.

Just as TQC provided workers with methods for approaching their work more scientifically, systems thinking provides managers with tools and a framework for continually testing and improving their decision making. By synthesizing these two methods into an integrated process, the Systemic Quality Management model captures the dual nature of managers' new work—rethinking issues and testing the outcomes on a conceptual as well as an operational level.

Daniel H. Kim is the publisher of The Systems Thinker™ *and director of the Learning Lab Research Project at the MIT Organizational Learning Center.*

Managing Organizational Learning Cycles

by Daniel H. Kim

I magine an organization in which all the records disintegrated overnight. Suddenly, there are no more reports, no computer files, no employee records, no operating manuals, no calendars—all that remain are the people, buildings, capital equipment, raw materials, and inventory. Now imagine an organization where all of the people have mysteriously disappeared. The organization is left intact in every other way, but there are no employees. Which organization will find it easier to rebuild its former status, to continue to take actions, and to learn?

One may be tempted to conclude that substituting new people would be easier than replacing all the information and systems. But even in the most bureaucratic organization, with all its standard operating procedures and established protocols, there is much more about the firm that is unsaid and unwritten. In fact, numerical and verbal databases only capture a small fraction of the information that is in mental "databases."

The essence of an organization is embodied in its people, not its systems. The intangible assets of a company reside in the individual mental models that contribute to the organization's memory. Without these mental models—which include the subtle interconnections that have been developed among the members—an organization will be incapacitated in both learning and action. Yet in most organizations, individual mental databases are not "backed up," nor is the transfer from individual to organizational learning well-managed. A critical challenge for a learning organization is understanding the transfer process through which individual learning and knowledge (mental models) become embedded in an organization's memory and structure. Once we have a clear understanding of this transfer process, we can actively manage organizational learning to be consistent with an organization's goals, vision, and values.

From Individual Learning...

In order to develop a framework for organizational learning, we must begin by understanding how individuals learn. The "Individual Learning Cycle" diagram shows a simplified model of individual learning. The diagram traces the process through which the brain assimilates some new data (environmental response), takes into account the memories of past experiences, comes to some conclusion about the new piece of information (individual learning), and then stores it away (individual mental models). After processing the new learning, one may choose to act or simply do nothing (individual action).

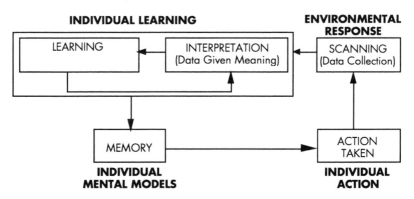

Adapted from Daft and Weick (1984)

Learning at the individual level can be described as a cycle in which the person assimilates new data, reflects on past experiences, draws a conclusion, and then acts.

The processing stage has been labeled "individual mental models" because it represents much more than the traditional concept of memory. Memory connotes a rather static repository for knowledge, whereas mental models involve the active creation of new knowledge. Mental models represent a person's view of the world, including both explicit and implicit understandings. They also provide the context in which to view and interpret new material, and they determine how stored information will be applied to a given situation.

...TO ORGANIZATIONAL LEARNING

In the early stages of an organization's existence, organizational learning is often synonymous with individual learning since it usually involves a very small group of people and the organization has minimal structure. As an organization grows, however, a distinction between the two levels of learning emerges. Somewhere in that process, a system evolves for capturing learnings from its individual members.

There is little agreement on what constitutes "appropriate" learning—those individual actions or learnings that should be transferred from the individual into the organization's memory. Standard operating procedures (SOPs), for example, are viewed as an important part of an organization's memory—a repository of past learning. But SOPs can also be a roadblock to learning if an organization becomes locked into old procedures and avoids searching for entirely new modes of behavior. How does an organization decide when once-appropriate routines are no longer valid? Can an organization anticipate obsolescence of its SOPs or must it always learn by first making inappropriate decisions in the face of changing conditions? These are the types of issues that a model of organizational learning must address.

ORGANIZATIONAL LEARNING CYCLES

By extending our model of individual learning to include organizational learning, we can begin to explore the transfer process between the two (see "A Simple Model of Organizational Learning"). This model represents the organizational learning cycle as a four-stage process, with organizational learning composed of three distinct sub-stages: individual learning, individual mental models, and organizational memory. Individual actions are taken based on individual mental models. These actions, in turn, translate into organizational action, and both actions produce some environmental response. The cycle is complete when the environmental response, in turn, leads to individual learning and affects individual mental models and organizational memory.

This simple model captures the transfer of individual learning to organizational memory via changes in individual mental models. Thus, organizational learning is separated from action (because all learning does not translate into taking new actions) and from environmental response (because all learning is not precipitated by the environment). The complete learning cycle, however, does include both the actions of the individual and the organization, as well as the environmental response to those actions.

A SIMPLE MODEL OF ORGANIZATIONAL LEARNING

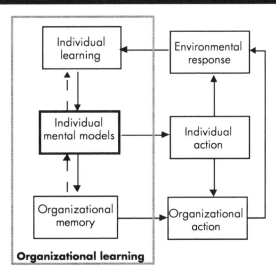

In this simple model of organizational learning, individual actions translate into organizational actions, producing some outcome (environmental response). The environmental response feeds back to affect individual learning, which in turn influences individual mental models and organizational memory.

Reflections on Creating Learning Organizations

An Integrated Model

There are at least two fundamentally different levels of learning at which an organization must be equally adept—operational and conceptual. *Operational learning* deals with the changes in the way we actually *do* things—filling out entry forms, operating a piece of machinery, handling a switchboard, re-tooling a machine, etc. While operational learning emphasizes the *how* of doing things, *conceptual learning* emphasizes the *why* of doing things—that is, it has do with the *thinking* behind why things are done in the first place. Conceptual learning deals with issues that challenge the very nature or existence of prevailing conditions or procedures. In order for organizational learning to be effective, however, conceptual learning must be operationalized into specific skills that can be learned and executed.

Individual Mental Models: Frameworks and Routines. Individual learning is captured in mental models through two different paths (see "Organizational Learning: An Integrated Model"). Operational learning produces new or revised routines that replace old or outworn ones. Conceptual learning leads to changes in frameworks, leading to new ways of looking at the world and new actions. For example, a design engineer may follow a six-step process for getting her drawings ready for a program review meeting. Through experience, she may learn to improve the process by streamlining some of the steps involved (operational learning). As she rethinks the *framework* of her work—the context in which the drawings are being produced and what their use is—she may question the production of the drawings themselves and identify situations when the drawings may not be necessary (conceptual learning). Her revised mental models will contain *both* the new frameworks and routines as well as the knowledge about how the routines fit within the new framework.

Organizational Memory: Weltanschauung and SOPs. The dual pathway continues from mental models to organizational memory. Over time, individual mental frameworks become embedded into the organization's own *weltanschauung*, or worldview. An organization's view of the world, in turn, affects how the individual interprets changes in the environment and how she translates her mental models into action. It also influences how the organization translates its organizational memory into action. For example, if an organization believes its ability to affect the environment is low, it will rely on standard routines and reactive behaviors. If, on the other hand, an organization assumes that it can take an active role in affecting its environment, this organization may approach everything in the spirit of experimentation, testing, and inventing.

In similar fashion, individual routines that are proven sound over

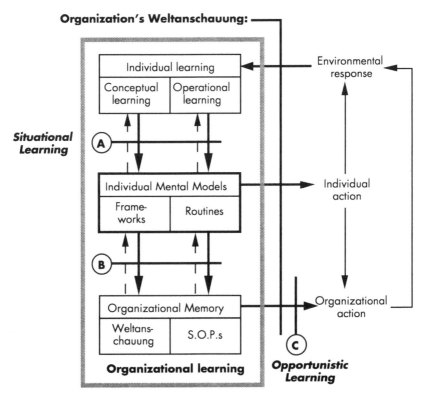

ORGANIZATIONAL LEARNING: AN INTEGRATED MODEL

Improving the organizational learning process means managing the whole cycle—individual learning, organizational learning, and the links between the two. At the same time, barriers to organizational learning (A, B, and C) must be addressed.

time become a company's standard operating procedures. The strength of the link between individual mental models and organizational memory depends how influential an individual or group is. In the case of a CEO or upper management, influence can be high due to the power inherent in the positions. Similarly, a united group of hourly workers can have a high degree of influence due to their size.

INCOMPLETE LEARNING CYCLES

Organizational learning requires completing the entire loop. If any of the links are either weak or broken, learning can be impaired. *Situational* learning, for example, occurs when the link between individual learning and individual mental models is severed: that is, the learning is situation-specific and does not change mental models. Crisis management is one example of situational learning in which each problem is solved but no learning is carried over to the next case.

When the link between individual models and organizational memory is broken, *fragmented* learning occurs. Individual mental models may change, but those changes are not reflected in the organization's memory. When organizational learning is fragmented among isolated individuals (or groups), the loss of the individuals (through turnover or layoffs) means loss of knowledge as well.

The link between organizational memory and organizational action, if broken, can lead to *opportunistic* learning. This occurs when organizational actions are pursued without taking into account organizational memory or the organization's values, culture, and SOPs. Sometimes this is done purposely, when one wishes to bypass the features of an organization that may impede progress on a specific front. The use of "skunk works" to develop the IBM personal computer is a good example, as is General Motors' entirely new car division, Saturn.

MANAGING THE WHOLE LEARNING CYCLE

Managing organizational learning means managing the complete cycle *explicitly*. Improving each of the pieces is not enough—the links between the pieces must also be managed. This requires addressing each of the incomplete learning cycles described above.

Beyond Situational Learning. Mental models are *the* critical pathway between individual learning and organizational memory. Mental models are the manager and arbiter of how new information will be acquired, retained, used, and deleted. Although a company can try to manage the flow of information, control the environment, or manipulate peoples' learning environment in various ways, if a person's view of the world remains unchanged, it is unlikely that any such actions will affect the quality of learning.

Therefore, closing the loop on situational learning—the link between individual learning and individual mental models—requires developing individuals' ability to transfer specific insights into more general maps that will guide them in the future. In order to make mental models explicit, we need appropriate tools to capture the type of knowledge that is being mapped.

Dynamic systems, in particular, require a different set of tools for making mental models explicit. Systems archetypes (systemic structures that recur repeatedly in diverse settings) such as "Shifting the Burden" and "Tragedy of the Commons" can be very helpful for eliciting and capturing managers' intuitive understanding of complex issues. *Action maps* are also useful for capturing the behavioral dynamics of a team or organization over time. They help managers see the larger patterns of behavior in which their specific actions are embedded. These two methods can help surface and capture a great deal of tacit individual knowledge in a way in which it can be shared, challenged, and subject to change—thus transferring it to organizational memory.

From Fragmented to Organizational Learning. Capturing individual mental models alone is not sufficient to achieve organizational learning, however. There also needs to be a way to prevent fragmented learning among individuals and to spread the learning throughout the organization. One way to accomplish this is through the design and implementation of *learning laboratories*—managerial practice fields where teams of managers can practice and learn together.

Learning laboratories can be designed, in part, around the learnings captured in systems archetypes and action maps. The spirit of the learning lab is one of active experimentation and inquiry, where everyone participates in surfacing and testing each other's mental models. Through this process, a shared understanding of the key assumptions and interrelationships of the organization can emerge. The use of an interactive computer management flight simulator offers the participants an opportunity to test their assumptions and to viscerally experience the consequences of their actions (see "'Flying' People Express Again," *The Systems Thinker*, Nov. 1990). The learning laboratory can be the vehicle through which organizational memory—via its weltanschauung and SOP's—can be enriched over time.

Harnessing Opportunistic Learning. If the organization's own culture and ways of doing things get in the way of learning, scenario planning and idealized designs can provide a way to break out of the norms. Royal Dutch Shell uses scenario planning to create alternative realities that stretch beyond what most managers in the company are likely to envision. By carefully constructing a multiple set of possible scenarios, Shell has been successful in anticipating and adapting to extremely volatile environments (see "Scenario-Based Planning: Managing by Foresight," *The Systems Thinker*, Dec. 1990/Jan. 1991).

Idealized designs, used by Russell Ackoff and his colleagues at INTERACT (Bala Cynwyd, PA), can also minimize the amount of influence an organization's current state has in determining its future. The principle idea is to start by crystallizing an ideal future without considering the current capabilities or organizational limitations. Thus, the planning process is "pulled" by where you want to be instead of "anchored" by where you are.

THE LEARNING CHALLENGE
The old model of a hierarchical corporation where the top thinks and the bottom acts is giving way to a new model where thinking and acting

must occur at all levels. As organizations push for flatter structures and reduced bureaucracy, there will be an increased reliance on the individuals to be the carriers of the organization's knowledge. Instead of codifying rules and procedures in handbooks and policy manuals, the new challenge is to continually capture the emerging understanding of the organization wherever it unfolds. At the heart of it all is understanding the role individual mental models play in the organizational learning cycle and continually finding ways to manage the transfer from individual to organizational learning.

Further reading: Daniel H. Kim, "Individual and Organizational Learning: Where the Twain Shall Meet?" System Dynamics Group Working Paper #D-4114 (MIT Sloan School of Management, Cambridge, MA) 1989.

Daniel H. Kim is the publisher of The Systems Thinker™ *and director of the Learning Lab Research Project at the MIT Organizational Learning Center.*

Paradigm-Creating Loops: How Perceptions Shape Reality

by Daniel H. Kim

We are in the midst of an unprecedented upheaval—a fundamental shift in the structure and nature of business. According to Fortune *magazine, "The greatest social convulsions of the years ahead may occur in the workplace, as companies struggling with fast-paced change and brutal competition re-shape themselves—and redefine what it means to hold a job" ("A Brave New Darwinian Workplace," Jan. 25, 1993).*

To respond to this changing paradigm, what is needed may not be a change of action, but a change in perception. How we think, act, and value is associated with our particular view of reality. In order to create a new "reality," we must discover how our current worldview affects the way we perceive and respond to problems. The leverage lies in going to a more fundamental level—to look beyond the problems themselves and re-examine the paradigm that gave rise to them.

The Problem-Solving Model of Managing

The prevailing model of management can be described as a "problem-solution" model: we encounter problems, and as managers, we are expected to solve them as quickly as possible (see "Problem Articulation"). In the "Problem-Solution Model," we attack each problem individually, apply an appropriate solution, and then move on to the next one.

The problems rarely remain "solved," however. From a systems thinking perspective, we can see how solutions often feed back to create *other* problems, or even a repeat of the same problem. By the time this happens, it often appears to be a brand new problem because we either have forgotten about the previous round of solutions, or the same person is no longer in that position (the average tenure in a position is 18 months

PROBLEM ARTICULATION

PROBLEM-SOLUTION MODEL

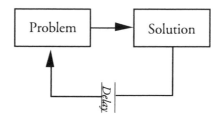

According to the "problem-solution" model, a problem occurs and a solution is applied that eliminates the problem. However, solutions often feed back to cause other problems, which can create a series of problem-solution cycles.

BALANCING PROBLEM ARTICULATION AND PROBLEM SOLVING

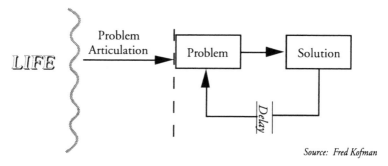

Source: Fred Kofman

To an extent, we create the problems we see by the way we view reality, and how we articulate those problems can determine the future direction of our reality. To break out of the "problem-solution" model of reality, we need to go back one step further to re-examine the question, "How did we distill out of this vast pool of life a particular problem which led us to act a certain way?"

or less in some companies). This creates a series of problem-solution cycles that can keep an organization continually busy fighting fires instead of taking more fundamental action.

At its worst, the problem-solution paradigm leads us to see problems in terms of predetermined solutions. Statements such as, "The problem is we need a better information system," or "The problem is we need the latest flexible manufacturing system," are examples of solution statements at work. The danger of this habit is that once we begin to frame problems in terms of solution statements, we exclude other possibilities—including the possibility that our original statement of the problem may be wrong.

Even when we don't resort to our favorite solution, we often don't challenge the problem statement itself. Problems are nothing more than a formal statement of a set of assumptions about the world. Those assumptions, however, are often not made explicit. By conversing and making decisions at the level of tacit assumptions, we can get very good at defending our point of view at the expense of learning. This can lead to what Chris Argyris of Harvard University calls "skilled incompetence." Rather than looking at the real data and real issues—which may prompt a re-articulation of the problem—we become very skilled at dancing around the issues.

PROBLEM ARTICULATION

To re-examine the way we think about problems and solutions, we need to understand more fundamentally what a problem is. In reality, there are no problems "out there" in the world—nature just *is*. Whether we see an event or situation as a problem depends on our view of the world. For example, if oil prices double, is that a problem? Our response would be a resounding "Yes!," since our economy is heavily dependent on petroleum products. If we lived in an OPEC nation, however, we would not see it as a problem at all. If we lived in an undeveloped country with no dependence on oil, we probably would not even be interested.

Problems do not exist independently of the person who sees them.

Out of the pool of life we "construct" problems in our minds (or in our organizations) by the way we view reality (see "Balancing Problem Articulation and Problem Solving"). Fred Kofman of the MIT Sloan School of Management suggests that deconstructing a problem and finding a way to re-articulate it can provide much more leverage than just trying to double our efforts to solve the problem as it is currently stated. One of the clear challenges is to explore more explicitly how we articulate problems. *Why* do we consider something a problem? The "why" is what leads us to surface the deeper set of assumptions that may give insight into reformulating an entirely different problem.

PARADIGM-CREATING LOOPS

How can we break out of the problem-solving straitjacket and begin reframing issues in new ways? One tool that can help is the "Ladder of Inference" developed by Chris Argyris. The "Ladder of Inference" provides a framework for exploring mental models. It graphically depicts the process we use to draw conclusive opinions and judgments from data, showing that individual evaluations are, in reality, highly abstract and inferential.

At the bottom of the "Ladder of Inference" is directly observable data: those things that can be objectively observed (see "The Reflexive Loop"). From that data, we add culturally shared meaning—that is, we interpret and make sense of an event by the norms of our culture. For example, suppose Bob, a colleague, walked into a 9:00 meeting at 9:15. The directly observable data is that Bob physically entered the room 15 minutes after the scheduled start time. What do we say to ourselves when we notice this? When managers are asked this question, typical responses are:

"He's late."

"He doesn't care."

"His previous meeting ran late."

"He's not a team player."

"He's disorganized."

If we locate the responses on the "Ladder of Inference," we see that most of them are on the higher rungs of the ladder, reflecting judgments and values based on the observable data.

There is nothing inherently wrong about drawing inferences and conclusions from the events we observe. In fact, the ability to move quickly up the ladder is what enables us to make sense of the incredibly complex, infinitely-detailed world in which we live. It is impossible for us to see and absorb everything—we are constantly selecting out a narrow slice of life to focus on and understand. What we don't often realize, however, is that our set of beliefs and assumptions directly affect the selection process by which we receive new observable data. Argyris calls this process the reflexive loop because it happens subconsciously and involuntarily.

THE REFLEXIVE LOOP

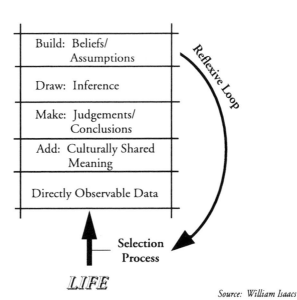

Source: William Isaacs

The reflexive loop illustrates how our mental models can influence the way we view reality. We make leaps up the "Ladder of Inference" from data to values and assumptions, and then operate based on those assumptions as if they are reality. It can also be called the paradigm-creating loop, because it is the process through which, over time, we develop a shared set of cultural assumptions and values about how we view reality.

For example, if we have concluded that Bob doesn't really care about meetings and is not a team player, what do we begin to notice about Bob? We take note of all the times he shows up late and we ignore or aren't aware of all the times he is on time. We notice that Bob does not say much at meetings, but don't register the fact that a few people always dominate the conversation and that there are others who say even less than Bob. We continually filter out any information that doesn't fit in with the mental model we have created about Bob. In fact, *all* the data we see confirm our beliefs and assumptions about Bob. We have leaped from data up to beliefs and assumptions, and then operated as if the assumptions *are* the reality.

The reflexive loop can also be called the paradigm-creating loop, because it is the process through which, over time, we develop a shared set of corporate assumptions and beliefs about reality. In *The Machine That Changed The World* (New York: Rawson Associates), there is a striking example of how this paradigm-creating process literally affects our ability to see. The book describes a new system of manufacturing invented by Toyota called "lean production" that uses less material, requires smaller inventories, has a shorter design time, and produces fewer defects than the traditional mass production system (See "Lean Production: From the Machine Age to the Systems Age," *The Systems Thinker,* August 1991). The authors tell the story of a General Motors plant manager's reaction after seeing a lean production plant in Japan: He "reported that secret repair areas and secret inventories had to exist behind the plant, because he hadn't seen enough of either for a 'real' plant." In actuality, there is no rework area in that plant—they drive the cars right off the assembly line and onto the ships. The GM manager's paradigm of a "real" plant kept him from seeing that there might be an alternative way to produce cars.

MISTAKING THE MAP FOR THE TERRITORY

Comedian Steven Wright tells this joke: "Last summer my wife and I were planning our summer vacation. We bought a map of the United

Encouraging diversity has become a prime objective in many organizations. As a result, it is fast becoming an unquestionable belief—oftentimes without a real understanding of its importance. Why should we value diversity? The implications of the reflexive loop suggest that each person has a completely unique perspective on the world—not just in a philosophical sense, but one that is actually grounded in the everyday experiences and worldview of the individual. In essence, the paradigm-creating loop is a world-creating loop. Each of us lives in an entirely unique world. We do have a great deal of overlap (i.e., culture) which allows us to interact and understand each other, but our uniqueness is a defining characteristic of who we are as an individual. Valuing diversity, then, allows us to access what each unique world has to offer. Having a diverse set of such worlds can create new possibilities and innovations that would otherwise not emerge.

States. It was life-sized. One mile equals one mile. We never went on the vacation because it took the whole summer to fold the map."

Of course, buying a life-sized map is ridiculous—it would be no more useful than reality itself. A map is useful precisely because it is a simplification of reality. We would never mistake the map for the territory and plan a trip as if California is only three feet away from New York. And yet we *are* prone to make such errors of perception whenever we mistake our mental models for the real world.

Marcel Proust once said, "The real voyage of discovery consists not in seeking new landscapes but in having new eyes." Becoming aware of how our view of the world is continually being constructed through the reflexive loop can prevent us from mistaking the map for the territory. Seeing problems as a product of our own thinking and not a product of nature can open our eyes to a whole new world of possibilities.

Further reading: Chris Argyris, "Teaching Smart People How to Learn," Harvard Business Review, *May/June 1991 (Reprint #91301).*

Daniel H. Kim is the publisher of The Systems Thinker™ *and director of the Learning Lab Research Project at the MIT Organizational Learning Center.*

Unlocking Organizational Routines that Prevent Learning

by Robert Putnam

Organizational life is awash with incongruities. In one organization the CEO told the world, "Product X is our top priority," even as the development group was putting it on the back burner. In another company, the unit that tracked product costs didn't communicate with the unit that set prices—although such costs are crucial for making good pricing decisions. In a third, a manager announced an open office arrangement to "improve communication." It was the first time the staff had heard of the idea.

In situations like these, the players are usually acting rationally from within their local perspectives—despite appearances to the contrary. Unfortunately, their reasoning is often not clear to others. Therefore, observers invent explanations such as "all he cares about is the stock price," "he's a typical sales guy," and "she's just trying to please the boss." These assumptions cannot be stated openly, but they influence how people act. Patterns then become established in which players unwittingly conspire to create behavior that is not in the best interest of the whole organization.

One reason these patterns persist is that individuals may not understand the effects of their behavior on the whole. And even when individuals do understand the whole, they may believe that they cannot act differently. A plant manager in the midst of a divisional downsizing program, for example, agreed that success would require redesigning work across several plants, not just within each plant. But he believed upper management would see organization-wide redesign as a delay tactic on his part to put off making cuts in his own plant. Therefore he continued to go along with a downsizing strategy that he believed was unwise.

To create organizations that learn, members must develop a shared understanding of how local rationalities interact to create organizational incongruities. Insight into each other's perspective reduces the escalation of private explanations that so often reinforce counterproductive patterns. It then becomes possible to see how one's own actions contribute to the problem—and to design solutions jointly that no one could implement alone.

COVERT BUDGETING

To further understand how these dynamics play out in corporations, consider a case of covert budgeting. The CEO of a large manufacturing company wished to reward individual initiative by connecting pay increases to performance. He was asked, "What if everyone in our department performs exceptionally well? Can we all get a large increase? Or will an individual receive more by being the one good performer in a department in which everyone else performs poorly?" The CEO responded that everyone should be treated as an individual. If every individual in a department—or in the company as a whole—performed exceptionally well, then everyone could get a large increase. Conversely, if no one performed exceptionally well, no one would get a large increase. Performance would therefore be the key.

This policy created difficulties for managers as they did their budgeting and salary planning, because the company tracked both how its compensation structure matched that of its competitors, and also how far each division was above or below a target compensation level. If a division was above its target, managers experienced pressure to hold the line on salary increases. And if the wage bill for the company as a whole increased too quickly, financial performance would, of course, suffer.

Therefore, each year senior management calculated what was a reasonable increase in the total wage bill and based employee compensation on that figure. Although the practice made sense, it was in direct conflict with the policy of rewarding individual performance independently of how others performed and were rewarded.

In this situation, each year first-level managers were asked to figure what salary increases they would recommend for each of their employees. These numbers were sent to second-level managers who added recommended increases for their subordinates and passed the results to third-level managers, and so on up the line. More often than not, when the results arrived at division management, the wage increases added up to more than could be allowed, so the numbers were sent back down for further work. Some years the yo-yo went through two or three cycles.

It did not take long for managers to realize that senior management had a particular wage target in mind (say a 5 percent increase). But managers were not told in advance what the number was that year. To tell managers a target number would let them duck responsibility for deciding what their people deserved, based on their performance. Not telling, of course, led to the considerable cost in managerial time of reworking the compensation numbers.

Managers knew there was a covert compensation budget, tried to second-guess what it was, and in fact *did* duck responsibility for compensation decisions by deferring to the budget. This came out when the CEO met with employees and asked, "What does your manager tell you when you do not get a pay increase?"

"Oh," was the reply, "he tells me the money isn't in the budget."

"But there isn't any budget for pay increases!" the CEO responded. Of course, on a *de facto* basis, there was a budget. But it is possible that the CEO did not know.

This case illustrates a central paradox of organizational learning: good members, acting rationally within the organizational world they know, create and maintain defensive routines that prevent the organization from learning. Defensive routines are habitual ways of interacting that serve to protect us or others from threat or embarrassment, but also prevent us from learning. Once they are started, these routines seem to take on a life of their own. Each player experiences them as an external force, imposed by the situation and by other actors. But they can actually be changed *only* by the players themselves. And change becomes likely only when players develop shared understanding of the interlocking dilemmas that lead them to act as they do (see "What Are Defensive Routines?").

DEFENSIVE ROUTINES

Defensive routines have probably existed for as long as there have been organizations. However, they take on an increasing importance in today's world for several reasons.

First, the pace of change in business today has put a premium on an organization's ability to learn. Therefore, routines that inhibit learning can no longer be tolerated.

Second, organizations must be able to integrate an increasing diversity of perspectives. Cultural, gender, and ethnic differences are but some of the drivers of diversity in how people think. Members of different professions, different functions, and different points in a supplier-customer chain can make unique contributions to shared understanding. However, defensive routines prevent us from taking advantage of multiple perspectives.

WHAT ARE DEFENSIVE ROUTINES?

Defensive routines are actions that...
- Prevent individuals and organizational units from experiencing embarrassment or threat.
- Simultaneously prevent people from identifying and changing the causes of the embarrassment or threat.
- Are taken for granted as "the ways things work."

Adapted from Argyris, 1990

Third, organizations are being designed to rely more on lateral and less on hierarchical links. Ironically, although command-and-control organizations may spawn defensive routines, they may also be able to function at an acceptable level despite them. It is when individuals must span lateral boundaries for the organization to function that it becomes essential to reduce routines that prevent mutual influence and learning.

CHARACTERISTICS OF DEFENSIVE ROUTINES

Defensive routines arise from a combination of behaviors and structures that interact to produce counterproductive and often alienating situations. We have accurate understanding only of our own circumstances; as a result, we are often unaware of how our actions affect others and how our behavior is part of a larger system. In this respect, defensive routines are like other systems that we find unmanageable; we only see small pieces of the puzzle and fail to realize how our well-intended actions create and maintain counterproductive patterns of behavior.

Because we cannot fully understand other people's positions, we often explain their behavior by attributing intentions that are based on our own assumptions. This human tendency becomes problematic when we focus on the difficulty that someone's behavior is creating for us and then go through a tacit chain of reasoning: They know they are having this impact... they intend it... it must be because they _____ (don't care, are protecting their turf, etc.). This logic makes it reasonable to hold others responsible for the problem.

Having made such attributions, we often try to conceal them. For example, if I believe that Jane is making a lame excuse to get out of meeting with me, I probably would not say that to her because it might create an argument. But this means that the attributions I make about Jane remain untested. Perhaps I decide that Jane is not interested in my work, so I do not invite her to the next meeting. Later Jane hears what I am doing and offers suggestions. But my project is so far along that using her ideas would require throwing out much of what I have done. "She wants influence," I think, "but she doesn't want to take the time. She's impossible." As we get more frustrated, angry, or discouraged in such situations, our untested attributions about others often begin to escalate.

On those rare occasions when routines are challenged, attributions and emotions are often expressed at an explosive level and the resulting discussion is counterproductive. These experiences confirm people's belief that it is best not to discuss the routines. As a result, defensive routines become undiscussable open secrets—and people begin to take their existence for granted. "Getting things done around here" begins to mean acting in ways that leave the routines in place.

If, for example, the executive committee has difficulty discussing conflictual issues, the CEO may choose to move those issues to a series of one-on-one meetings. While bypassing defensive routines may be necessary for short-term progress, it often reinforces the routines for the longer term. With the conflictual issues safely off the agenda, the executive committee becomes even more incapable of dealing with the important business of the firm.

Using Action Maps to Unlock Defensive Routines

To reduce defensive routines, we need to recognize what maintains the routines. How people think as they design actions—making assumptions and attributing intentions to others, keeping their attributions private, and acting on the basis of that untested thinking—all contribute to defensive routines. We can actually think of defensive routines as systemic structures whose causal links are embedded in the mental models of the players.

Therefore we might try to reduce the grip those routines have by helping people reflect on the mental models that drive their actions. While this is an essential step, it is not usually the best place to start, since most people do not see a pressing need to change their mental models. Working on mental models makes sense only *after* it becomes clear that the work is necessary in order to make progress on organizational responsibilities.

A more effective approach to addressing defensive routines is to start by exploring key organizational objectives that members are having difficulty achieving. Individuals are asked to identify the barriers to achieving their objectives by describing examples and illustrating how they or others have tried to manage the barriers. This information becomes the basis for discussion in a group or management team.

One way to organize this information is in action maps that show how different players think and act in ways that unintentionally contribute to defensive routines. By displaying the interlocking dilemmas of each party and how their actions reinforce each other, the maps can counteract the tendency to polarize. Organizational dilemmas are most often managed by each group grabbing one horn. They pull in different directions, each seeing clearly that the other way lies disaster. But the essence of a dilemma is that either horn leads to trouble. Maps can actually help groups embrace the whole dilemma and work from there. They also puncture the undiscussability that maintains defensive routines. By identifying the contribution of each party to unintended results, maps reduce the tendency to pin blame rather than to work together.

THE FORECASTING GAME ACTION MAP

The "Forecasting Game Action Map" (see diagram) was designed to make the difficulties experienced by a management group visible and discussible. The group identified their forecasting process as a key barrier to making sound resource allocation decisions. While the map was based specifically on the information derived from that organization, individuals from several different organizations have since confirmed that it describes what happens in their worlds as well.

The "game" works this way. People in divisions wish to ensure that they will be able to make or beat their forecast. As forecasting is an inherently uncertain enterprise, to ensure beating the forecast it is necessary to leave a safety margin by overstating anticipated expenses or understating anticipated revenues (perhaps by using assumptions that are known to be conservative). These tactics, however, are inconsistent with the stated obligation to give corporate a forecast that is as accurate as possible, and therefore it must be kept private. If the division does not appear to be a good "corporate citizen," corporate would have legitimate reason to impose sanctions. Therefore, the fact that there are safety margins and that they are being kept private must be hidden as well. How? By acting as if nothing is being hidden.

From corporate's point of view, accurate information is essential for guiding management action. But corporate officers are not naive; they know divisions often hedge by keeping private safety margins. There-

FORECASTING GAME ACTION MAP

Division Thinking
- Make sure we can beat the forecast
- Must look like good corporate citizen

Division Action
- Keep private safety margin
- When squeezed, give up minimal amount

Consequences
- The harder corporate squeezes, the more division thinks it must hold back and cover up
- The more division holds back, the harder corporate thinks it must squeeze

Each feels reinforced in own approach.

Corporate Thinking
- Need accurate numbers to drive corrective action
- Divisions usually hedge

Corporate Action
- Apply pressure to reduce hidden safety margin
- Require detail so can discover offsets and hedging

Source: Robert Putnam

The "Forecasting Game Action Map" makes explicit the "local rationalities" that led to actions taken by both the division and corporate, and shows how the unintended consequences of those actions lock both players into a counterproductive dynamic.

fore corporate officers apply pressure, telling divisions to rework the numbers to reduce costs or increase revenues, or they may pose sharp questions or require detailed information in an effort to discover where safety margins may be hidden.

When corporate squeezes, divisions know they must often "give" a little bit on their numbers. They try to give the minimal amount that will satisfy corporate while still leaving an adequate safety margin. Of course, the fact that divisions give something reinforces corporate's efforts to squeeze ("See, they were able to do more than they had said"). On the other hand, the established pattern of "squeezing and giving" reinforces the need for divisions to create private safety margins: they must build in some extra cushion so they will be able to give when they are squeezed and yet still have something left over. Each side feels reinforced in its approach.

This pattern, or a variation on it, is an open secret in many organizations. Not only does it contaminate the forecasting process, but it also contributes to a culture of ritual deception. Yet most players within the "Game" are actually striving to act responsibly and do a good job. Many dislike participating in deception, but feel they have no choice. Others have become inured to the process or have created rationalizations to justify their actions. All of them are locked into a recurring pattern that will continue unless they jointly work to change it.

DISCUSSING ACTION MAPS

Discussing a map of one's own defensive routines can be both a liberating and difficult experience. It can be liberating because most of us dislike living open secrets. All of the players involved are familiar with the Forecasting Game; being presented with a map simply makes it legitimate to talk about the issues. And it becomes possible to design change actions that were not possible as long as the situation could not be discussed. For example, players might agree on legitimate reasons for conservative forecasting. Divisions might make the reasoning underlying their forecasts more transparent to corporate, and corporate might allow some degree of hedging against uncertainty.

But talking about defensive routines can be difficult for all the reasons that they are usually kept undiscussable. Habits of thought persist that lead people to make attributions about others, to get upset about it, and to remain blind to the legitimacy of other perspectives. For example, administrators at the director level of a public agency were talking about the pressures that led them not to share as much budget information as staff wanted. An administrator one or two levels lower listened as long as he could and then burst out, "You're all making excuses! I know you could share more information if you wanted to!" Comments like this can easily escalate into a polarized discussion that inhibits inquiry and reflection—and reinforces the very defensive routines that are being discussed.

Open discussion about defensive routines can improve mutual understanding and create shared commitment to reducing the routines. Implementing new actions, however, often requires developing the skill to act differently under stress. Telling an executive that he or she is contributing to defensive routines may be a tall order. It is at this point that it makes sense to introduce concepts and techniques for creating learning conversations. Once we understand how current, taken-for-granted ways of acting create defensive routines that prevent achieving organizational objectives, members may be ready to commit to practicing new ways of acting.

Further reading: The underlying theory of defensive routines was developed by Chris Argyris and is presented in his book Overcoming Organizational Defenses, *published by Allyn & Bacon, 1990). Argyris' most recent book,* Knowledge For Action *(Jossey-Bass, 1993) describes in detail how an organization worked to reduce defensive routines. Both are available through Pegasus Communications.*

Robert Putnam is a partner in Action Design, a consulting firm based in Newton, MA. He is co-author with Chris Argyris and Diana McLain Smith of Action Science *(Jossey-Bass, 1985).*

Human Dynamics:
A Foundation for the
Learning Organization

by Sandra Seagal and David Horne

In *The Fifth Discipline*, Peter Senge posed the question, "How can a team of committed managers with individual IQs above 120 have a collective IQ of 63?"

One reason is that each team member brings to the group fundamental differences in his or her way of working and seeing that are usually not recognized and accommodated. These differences can create discomfort or conflict that consumes energy rather than releasing it for creativity and new learning. When the differences are known and understood, however, they can be utilized for superior team functioning.

For example, imagine that a four-person team has been assigned the task of creating a human resource development training program for their organization. It becomes clear from the outset that each member has a distinctly different point of view. Even before they get into the assignment, one team member wants definitions—he wants to know precisely what is meant by the terms "human resources" and "development," and what the long-term purpose of the training is.

Another person believes it is more critical to know what has been done in the past—she wants more data to set the context for considering next steps. She asks what has worked in the past and what the measurable results have been.

The third member of the group is most focused on assessing and promoting the comfort level of each team member, including himself. He wants to feel that the group is harmonized before they discuss the task. He is concerned with the individual relevance of the proposed program, and the personal implications for the people who will participate in it.

Finally, the fourth member of the team simply wants to move forward. She can't understand why the team doesn't just *begin* with something innovative and untested. It is evident to her that human resources requires sustained development, so she thinks, "Why all the discussion? Let's put out some ideas and take some action."

As each team member works to resolve his or her own needs, conflict builds within the group. None of the members can understand why the others are not "hearing" them. The frustration gradually builds until it reaches a point at which the group may not be able to address the task effectively.

HUMAN DYNAMICS

Underneath the dynamics described above are some fundamental distinctions in the way people function. The study of Human Dynamics, which began in 1979 and has involved more than 40,000 people from over 25 cultures, is devoted to understanding these distinctions. It has resulted in new awareness—both of individuals' unique personality systems and of the interactions of these systems in the larger contexts of the family, the classroom, the workplace, and the community. With such an understanding, we can begin to build on the synergy of different learning processes to enhance our dialogues and to create more effective teams and organizations.

THE CORE UNIVERSAL PRINCIPLES

Human Dynamics focuses on exploring the interaction of three universal principles: the mental, the emotional (or relational), and the physical (or practical). Each of these principles is critical in the development of a complete and balanced person.

The mental principle in the human system is related to the mind—to thinking, values, structure, focus, objectivity, and perspective. The emotional principle is more subjective. It is concerned with relationships—with communication, organization, feelings, and putting things together in new ways (creativity). The physical principle is pragmatic. It is the making, doing, and operationalizing part of ourselves.

These three principles combine in nine possible variations to form distinct ways of functioning, which we term "personality dynamics." Five of these personality dynamics predominate in Western cultures, while two of the five predominate in the Far East. Each constitutes a whole way of functioning, characterized by distinctive processes of learning, communicating, problem-solving, relating to others, contributing to teams, maintaining well-being, and responding to stress. Each has

THREE UNIVERSAL PRINCIPLES

MENTAL	EMOTIONAL	PHYSICAL
Thinking	Feeling	Making
Objectivity	Subjectivity	Doing
Vision	Relationship	Actualizing
Overview	Communication	Sensory Experience
Structure	Organization	Practicality
Values	Creative Imagination	

Human Dynamics focuses on exploring the interaction of three universal principles: the mental, the emotional (or relational), and the physical (or practical). These three principles combine in nine possible variations to form distinct ways of functioning.

distinctive ways of handling change, and each has a characteristic path of development.

The personality dynamics appear in every culture, characterize males and females equally, and can be observed at every age level. One of the many distinguishing features of the Human Dynamics perspective is that it is possible to identify the personality dynamic in childhood, even in infancy, thus providing invaluable information for parents and teachers on the specific educational and developmental needs of their children and students. Part of the research has involved tracking the development of children over the course of many years. The personality dynamic remains consistent over time, but is expressed with increasing maturity.

It is essential to understand that Human Dynamics is a developmental paradigm. Every personality dynamic has an embedded capac-

A DISTINCT WHOLE SYSTEM

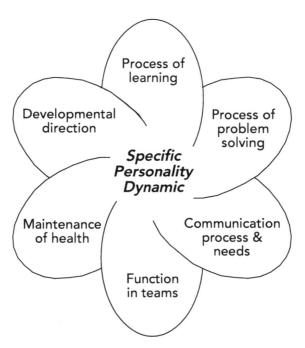

Each personality dynamic constitutes a distinct whole system of functioning.

ity for maturation, though the path of development toward wholeness is distinct for each. A spiritual dimension, termed the Deep Capacity, is also recognized. Maturation involves integration and development of the mental, emotional, and physical aspects of each personality dynamic, and fuller expression of the Deep Capacity.

Another distinctive feature of the Human Dynamics approach is that no testing is required. People identify their own personality dynamic through a process of discovery, and are helped to recognize the personality dynamics of others through sensitive observation and participation.

It is important to note that each personality dynamic is of equal value. Anyone of any personality dynamic may be more or less intelligent, compassionate, skilled, or gifted. It is the *way* in which each dynamic functions that is entirely distinct.

The implications of recognizing these distinctions for the development of learning communities is profound. People really do learn, communicate, relate, and develop in fundamentally different ways. Awareness and understanding of the distinctions offer new opportunities for self-understanding and growth; for improved communication and positive relationships; and for teamwork that utilizes the gifts of each member in conscious synergy. Each whole system potentially complements the others, enhancing the overall functioning of a team or organization.

PERSONALITY DYNAMICS

Below are thumbnail sketches of each of the five predominant personality dynamics, with particular emphasis on their functioning in teams:

Mentally Centered. The mentally centered plan from the top down, from the abstract to the particular, and back again. They usually have a gift for long-range perspective and for logical planning to achieve long-term goals. They ask the essential questions, often beginning with "Why?"

Their sensitivity to basic principles and precepts enables them to offer "course correction" should a group begin to stray from its purpose or vision. Because of their natural objectivity and affinity for perspective, they are often able to articulate the principle or overarching consideration that unifies seemingly disparate views.

However, they may often be silent in a group. One reason for this is that they typically feel no need to articulate a point if someone else is making it. Also, because they process internally, think logically, and like to articulate their point of view precisely, they may have difficulty finding space to contribute in a less orderly group process. Their silence should not be interpreted as aloofness or non-involvement. They can be helped to contribute if asked questions.

Phrases commonly used by mentally centered people include: "What exactly is the purpose?" "What are the long-term implications?" "What exactly do you mean by...?"

Emotional-Mental (also called Emotional-Objective.) Emotional-objective people are emotional about their ideas, which they often express with great intensity. One of the main functions of this group is to initiate; they light the fires of new endeavors. Movement is their inner directive. They want to establish the direction of a task, its purpose and value, and then move into action as soon as possible, learning as they go. They are usually adept at creating beginning structures that allow a process to take form.

Theirs is a brainstorming, experimental, open-ended "R&D" process in which new possibilities and lines of inquiry are offered and explored, typically directed toward the short-term future. It is often assumed that this group wants to "take charge," when in fact they are usually simply living their natural function of breaking new ground.

The processing of emotional-objective people is primarily external—they think on their feet. In teams, this group frequently begins the discussion, facilitates the interplay of ideas, and wants to keep the process moving forward. Phrases you may hear from emotional-objective people include: "Let's put all the ideas on the board and prioritize." "The details can wait—first let's create a general structure." "It's good enough." "Let's go!"

Emotional-Physical (also called Emotional-Subjective). Emotional-subjective people respond to tasks (as to all of life) in a personal way. They *feel* the personal implications of any undertaking, both for themselves and for others who may be involved or affected. In order to explore, understand, and become comfortable with these implications, they need time to engage in extensive intrapersonal and interpersonal processing. They require dialogue that involves exploring their own feelings and those of others, as well as related personal experiences, while at the same time dealing with the problem or assignment itself. They learn most readily through interpersonal exchange.

RHYTHM IN THE PROCESS OF COMMUNICATION

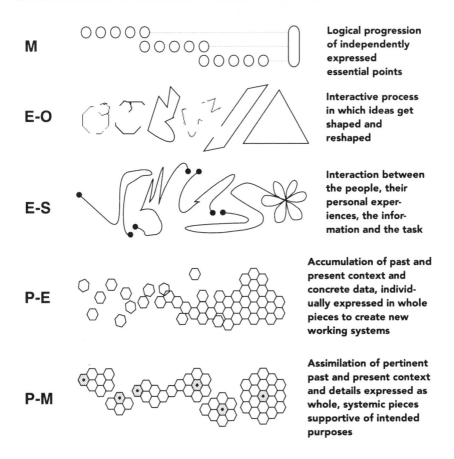

M — Logical progression of independently expressed essential points

E-O — Interactive process in which ideas get shaped and reshaped

E-S — Interaction between the people, their personal experiences, the information and the task

P-E — Accumulation of past and present context and concrete data, individually expressed in whole pieces to create new working systems

P-M — Assimilation of pertinent past and present context and details expressed as whole, systemic pieces supportive of intended purposes

One of the core motivations of emotional-subjective people is to create and sustain harmony. In a team situation they therefore have a double task—that of maintaining group harmony while simultaneously addressing the team's purposes and issues. Emotional-subjective people are usually highly insightful regarding the "people issues" involved. They are highly intuitive, but are not always able to explain these feelings rationally in the moment. Given time for processing, the emotional-subjective person will usually come to a rational understanding of his/her intuition and be able to recommend an appropriate action. The intuitive capacities and creative skills of emotional-subjective people are natural resources that organizations often waste.

Phrases that are familiar to emotional-subjective people are: "Is that comfortable for you?" "I need time to process before I can take another step." "My gut feeling is...".

Physical-Emotional. Physical-emotional people are natural systems thinkers. In any undertaking, they spend the longest time gathering data, assimilating and synthesizing it—in an organic process that mostly takes place internally, and takes its own time. The result, if sufficient time is allowed, is a plan or product that is detailed, comprehensive, and systemically linked.

In teams, physical-emotional members are often people of few words, preferring communication that is factual, down-to-earth, and pragmatic. It is sometimes difficult for them to contribute to a team process if the pace is not sufficiently deliberate, but because they see and think in terms of whole systems, they may have a great deal to say on any particular issue if they are given the opportunity. They absorb enormous amounts of factual information, and their capacity to remember detail is usually prodigious. They are capable of summing up the content of any meeting because they are natural recorders of everything said. However, they may not be ready to give their conclusions regarding the meeting until a later occasion, when they have had time to assimilate all that has occurred.

Phrases you might hear from a physical-emotional person include:

"I need some sense of the parameters." "Can you give me more context?" "We need to expose them to the actual experience, not just talk about it."

Physical-Mental. The physical-mental group shares many of the characteristics of the physical-emotional group. They, too, are pragmatic, need a considerable amount of context, and take in a great deal of information. However, they are more selective of the data they take in and begin to structure it more quickly around the purpose, which they want to clearly establish from the beginning. Like the physical-emotional, they think and plan systemically, but in less detail. They therefore tend to move to action more quickly.

Like the mentally centered, they have natural gifts for objectivity, structure, and long-range strategic planning. Unlike the mentally centered, however, they tend to work from the concrete to the abstract—from current reality to future outcomes—so they gather more factual detail. Phrases you might hear from a physical-mental person include: "What is the purpose?" "What is the current reality?" "Let's make a model to clarify this...".

HUMAN DYNAMICS AND THE FIVE DISCIPLINES
Human Dynamics provides a foundation of human understanding and development that facilitates implementation of each of the five disciplines identified by Peter Senge as crucial in building learning communities.

Systems Thinking. Human Dynamics offers the opportunity for including in any process the most fundamental system of all, the human system. Human Dynamics looks at *people* as distinct learning systems. Each individual is acknowledged as representing a specific whole system of mental, emotional, physical, and spiritual interaction and expression. Further, each personality dynamic system is recognized as functioning as an essential component of an interactive system that includes *all* of the personality dynamics. Not only are the needs and gifts and processes of all of the individual personality dynamics taken into account, but so is their dynamic complementarity. Groups on any scale, whether a family unit, project team, organization, or even the human race, can be viewed as a system of interaction of the different personality dynamics.

Mental Models. Human Dynamics demonstrates how each of the personality dynamics operates from a fundamentally distinct experiential base. Therefore, each brings to any discussion or endeavor a specific perspective and set of assumptions that differ from those of the other personality dynamics. One purpose of the Human Dynamics work is to make these distinctions clear, so that an individual's words or actions can be understood in the context of that person's basic "way of being." This helps assure greater mutual understanding and more empathic communication.

Personal Mastery. Every aspect of Human Dynamics is concerned with personal mastery, beginning with the most essential requisite of all—knowledge of oneself. Human Dynamics programs involve a voyage of discovery—about oneself, others, and the different processes of communication, problem-solving, learning, and developing, and about what can be done in light of these discoveries to optimize how we live and learn and work together.

Shared Vision. The quality of a shared vision depends upon the visionary capacity of the individual participants. From the perspective of Human Dynamics, the capacity for vision is an attribute of the mental principle. However, the vision must also include people's needs (emotional principle) and a way to bring the vision into being (physical principle). Combining exercises for the development of the three principles in a visioning session can produce a much more inclusive and qualitative personal or collective vision, in which head, heart, deep aspiration, and actualizing intent are all represented.

Team Learning. Awareness and understanding of the different personality dynamics is an essential ingredient in qualitative team functioning.

The team developing the human resource training program, for example, would have begun their process at a completely different place of understanding, respect, and empowerment if they had had a framework for understanding each other's ways of learning and operating. This particular team was fortunate to have the diversity of perspective of one mentally centered, one physical-emotional, one emotional-subjective, and one emotional-objective person. However, without a framework for understanding and integrating their distinct gifts so as to achieve a common goal, the group became mired in a frustrating and unproductive process.

Not only can existing teams learn to function more harmoniously and productively, but balanced teams can be consciously assembled in which the various personality dynamics are all represented. As many organizations are currently discovering, such a team can turn its attention to almost anything with success because the results will integrate the natural gifts and way of seeing of each of the personality dynamics.

When teams (or families, groups, or communities) are *conscious* of the distinctions, the differences become assets rather than liabilities, and the performance of the team indeed becomes greater than the sum of its parts.

Human Dynamics programs are currently being disseminated in the fields of business, education, healthcare, and community development.

Sandra Seagal is founder and president of Human Dynamics International (Topanga, CA) and executive director of Human Dynamics Foundation. Both organizations are devoted to the development, empowerment, and sustainment of individual and collective human potential. David Horne has been involved in the development of Human Dynamics since 1983.

DIALOGUE: THE POWER OF COLLECTIVE THINKING

by William Isaacs

"There is a beginning to dialogue, but I do not think there is an end."
—president of a local Steelworkers Union

The way people talk together in organizations is rapidly becoming acknowledged as central to the creation and management of knowledge. According to Alan Webber, former editor of the *Harvard Business Review*, conversation is the means by which people share and often create what they know. Therefore, "the most important work in the new economy is creating conversations" ("What's So New About the New Economy?," *Harvard Business Review*, Jan.-Feb. 1993). Dialogue, the discipline of collective learning and inquiry, is a process for transforming the quality of conversation and the thinking that lies beneath it.

THE POWER OF DIALOGUE

Complex issues require intelligence beyond that of any individual. Yet in the face of complex, highly-conflictual issues, teams typically break down, revert to rigid positions, and cover up deeper views. The result: watered-down compromises and tenuous commitment. Dialogue, however, is a discipline of collective learning and inquiry. It can serve as a cornerstone for organizational learning by providing an environment in which people can reflect together and transform the ground out of which their thinking and acting emerges.

Dialogue is not merely a strategy for helping people talk together. In fact, dialogue often leads to new levels of coordinated action without the artificial, often tedious process of creating action plans and using consensus-based decision making. Dialogue does not require agreement; instead it encourages people to participate in a pool of shared meaning, which leads to aligned action.

Since 1992, The Dialogue Project at MIT has been conducting a series of practical experiments to create dialogue and explore its impacts. While it is still at an early stage, we have witnessed moving and, at times, profound changes in the individuals and groups with which we have worked. For example, labor and management representatives from a steel mill have discovered dramatic shifts in their ways of thinking and talking together. In a recent presentation by this dialogue group, one union participant said, "We have learned to question fundamental categories and labels that we have applied to each other."

"Can you give us an example?" one manager asked.

"Yes," he responded, "labels like management and union."

This particular group has transformed a 50-year-old adversarial relationship into one where there is genuine and serious inquiry into "taken-for-granted" ways of thinking. The steelworkers, for example, recognized that they had far more in common with management than they had previously realized or expected. "We quit talking about the past," said the union president. "We didn't bring any of that up, all the hurt and mistrust that we've had over the last twenty years." Another steelworker noticed that the category "union" limited him as much as it protected him. "It's important to suspend the word 'union,'" he said.

In another setting, we brought together major health care providers for a city—hospital CEOs, doctors, nurses, insurance agents, technicians, and a legislator—to create a microcosm of the healthcare system. This group has been inquiring into some of the underlying assumptions and forces that seem to make this field so chaotic.

In one session, participants confronted the collective pain felt when assuming responsibility for all the illnesses of a community. One senior physician said, "I am struck by my schizophrenia: the difference between how I treat my patients and how I treat all of you." This dialogue has begun to surface the underlying sources of counter-productivity inherent in the healthcare system. In the past, people have sought self-protection against such pain, but this has led to costly isolation, misplaced competitiveness, and lack of coordination.

DIA • LOGOS

Dialogue can be defined as a sustained collective inquiry into the processes, assumptions, and certainties that structure everyday experience. The word "dialogue" comes from two Greek roots, *dia* and *logos*, suggesting "meaning flowing through." This is in marked contrast to what we frequently call dialogue—a mechanistic and unproductive debate between people seeking to defend their views. Dialogue actually involves a willingness not only to suspend defensive exchange but also to probe into the reasons for it. In this sense, dialogue is a strategy aimed at resolving the problems that arise from the subtle and pervasive fragmentation of thought (see "Fragmentation of Thought").

FRAGMENTATION OF THOUGHT

Fragmentation of thought is like a virus that has infected every field of human endeavor. Drawing in part upon a worldview inherited from the 16th century (which saw the cosmos as a giant machine), we have divided our experience into separate, isolated bits. Nowhere does this fragmentation become more apparent than when human beings seek to communicate and think together about difficult issues. Rather than reason together, people defend their "part," seeking to win over others.

Recent developments in quantum theory and cognitive science indicate that this reductionist perspective is a fictitious way of thinking. The discovery of what Niels Bohr called "quantum wholeness" suggests that, at the quantum level, we cannot separate the observer and the observed. For example, light can behave like a particle or a wave depending on how you set up the experiment. What you perceive, in other words, is a function of how you try to perceive that reality. As physicist David Bohm put it, "the notion that all these fragments are separately existent is evidently an illusion, and this illusion cannot do other than lead to endless conflict and confusion."

Physicist David Bohm has compared dialogue to superconductivity. In superconductivity, electrons cooled to very low temperatures act more like a coherent whole than as separate parts. They flow around obstacles without colliding with one another, creating no resistance and very high energy. At higher temperatures, however, they begin to act like separate parts, scattering into a random movement and losing momentum.

Particularly when discussing tough issues, people act more like separate, high-temperature electrons. Dialogue seeks to help people attain high energy and low friction without ruling out differences between them. Negotiation tactics, in contrast, often try to cool down interactions by bypassing the most difficult issues and narrowing the field of exchange to something manageable. They achieve "cooler" interactions, but lose energy and intelligence in the process. In dialogue, the aim is to create a special environment in which a different kind of relationship among the parts can come into play—one that reveals both high energy and high intelligence.

THE PRACTICE OF DIALOGUE

The pivotal challenge lies in producing dialogue in practical settings. Dialogue poses a paradox in practice. While it seeks to allow greater coherence among a group of people (note this does not necessarily imply *agreement*), it does not impose it. Indeed, dialogues surface and explore the very mechanisms by which people try to control and manage the meanings of their interactions.

People often come to a dialogue with the intention of understanding their fundamental concerns in a new way. Yet in contrast with more familiar modes of inquiry, it is helpful to begin without an agenda, without a "leader" (although a facilitator is essential) and without a task or decision to make. By deliberately not trying to solve problems in a familiar way, dialogue opens a new possibility for shared thinking.

One story illustrates the power of this kind of exchange. In the late 1960s, the dean of a major U.S. business school was appointed to chair a committee to examine whether the university, which had major government contracts, should continue to design and build nuclear bombs on campus. People were in an uproar over the issue. The committee was somewhat like Noah's ark: two of every species of political position on the campus. The chairman had no idea how to bring all these people together to agree on anything, so he changed some of the rules. The committee would meet, he said, *every day* until it had produced a report. Every day meant exactly that—weekends, holidays, everything. People objected, but he persisted.

The group eventually met for 36 days straight. Critically, for the first two weeks, they had no agenda. People just talked about anything they wanted to talk about: the purpose of the university, how upset they were, their deepest fears, and their noblest aims. They eventually turned to the report they were supposed to write. By this time, they had become quite close. In the corner you might have seen two people conferring who previously had intensely clashing views. To the surprise of many, the group eventually produced a unanimous report. What was striking was they agreed on a direction, *but for different reasons*. They did not need to have the same reasons to agree with the direction that emerged.

LEVELS AND STAGES OF DIALOGUE

Dialogue requires creating a series of increasingly-conscious environments in which a special kind of "cool inquiry" can take place. These environments, which we call "containers," can develop as a group of people become aware of the requirements and discipline needed to create them (see "Initial Guidelines for Dialogue"). A container can be understood as the sum of the assumptions, shared intentions, and beliefs of a group. These create a collective "atmosphere" or climate. The core of the theory of dialogue builds on the premise that changes in people's shared attention can alter the quality and level of inquiry that is possible.

The evolution of a dialogue among a group of people consists of

INITIAL GUIDELINES FOR DIALOGUE

- Suspend Certainties
- Listen to Your Listening
- Slow Down the Inquiry
- Be Aware of Thought
- Maintain Peripheral Attention

both levels and stages. They tend to be sequential, although once one moves through a stage, one can return to it (see "Evolution of Dialogue"). Passing through a level usually involves facing different types of individual and collective crises. The process is demanding, and at times frustrating, but also deeply rewarding.

1. INSTABILITY *OF* THE CONTAINER

When any group of individuals comes together, each person brings a wide range of tacit, unexpressed differences in paradigms and perspectives. The first challenge in a dialogue is to recognize this, and to accept that the purpose of the dialogue is not to hide them, but to find a way of allowing the differences to be explored. These implicit views are often inconsistent with one another. Since we generally deal with inconsistencies in rigid and mechanistic ways, the "container" or environment for dialogue at this stage is unstable.

Dialogue begins with conversation (the root of the word means "to turn together"). People begin by speaking together, and from that flows deliberation ("to weigh out"). Consciously and unconsciously people weigh out different views, agreeing with some and disliking others. They selectively pay attention, noticing some things, missing others.

At this point people face the first crisis and choice of the dialogue process, one that can either lead to the further refinement and evolution of the dialogue environment, or can lead to greater instability. This "initiatory crisis" occurs as people recognize that despite their best intentions, *they cannot force dialogue.* People find they cannot comprehend, much less impose coherence, on the diversity of views. They must choose either to defend their point of view, or *suspend* (not *sup-*

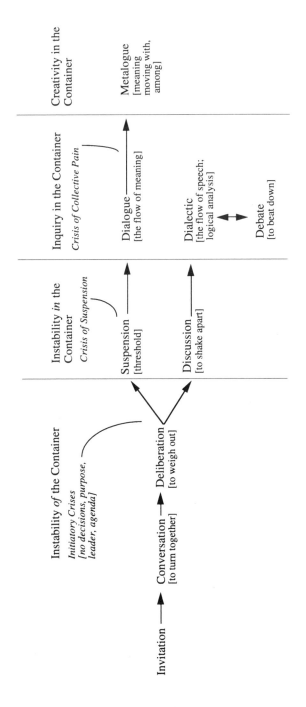

press) their view and begin to listen without judgment, loosening the grip of certainty about all views (including their own).

2. INSTABILITY *IN* THE CONTAINER

A recognition of this "initiatory" crisis begins to create an environment in which people know they are seeking to do something different. At this point, groups often begin to oscillate between suspending views and discussing them. People will feel the tendency at this point to fall into the familiar habit of analyzing the parts, instead of focusing on the whole.

At this stage, people may find themselves feeling frustrated. Others may defend their views despite evidence that they may be wrong. They may make definitive statements about what is or is not happening, but fail to explore their assumptions or other possibilities. They may see their behavior as a function of how others think and act, and discount their own responsibility for it. Normally all of this is either taken for granted or kept below the surface. But in dialogue we deliberately seek to make these general patterns of thought observable and accessible and surface the tacit influences that sustain them.

At this point in the dialogue people begin to see and explore the range of assumptions that are present. They ask: Which are true? Which are false? How far is the group willing to go to expose itself? This leads to a second crisis, namely the "crisis of suspension." Points of view that used to make sense no longer do. The direction of the group is unclear. Some people experience disorientation or perhaps feel marginalized and constrained by others. Polarization occurs as extreme views become stated and defended. The fragmentation that has been hidden is appearing, now in the container.

For example, in an ongoing dialogue with a group of labor and management representatives from a steel mill, the "same old kind" of conflicts emerged. Some participants felt helpless and defeated, others went "ballistic." Yet they did not walk out. They stayed to explore the ways in which they had all contributed to the unproductive dynamics. Likewise, in the healthcare dialogue, suppressed conflict, anger, and long-time simmering "myths" about one another began to surface.

To manage the crisis of collective suspension, everyone must be aware of what is happening. Rather than panic, withdraw, or fight, people may choose to inquire. Listening here is not just listening to others, but listening to oneself. And people may ask: Where am I listening from? What can I learn if I slow things down and inquire?

Skilled facilitation is critical at this point. The facilitator, however, is not seeking to "correct" or impose order on what is happening, but to show how to suspend what is happening to allow greater insight into the order that is present. The facilitator might point out the polarization and the limiting categories of thought that are rapidly gaining momentum in the group.

3. INQUIRY IN THE CONTAINER

If a critical mass of people stay with the process beyond this point, the conversation begins to flow in a new way. In this "cool" environment people begin to inquire together as a whole. New insights often emerge. The energy that had been trapped in rigid and habitual patterns of thought and interaction begins to be freed.

When we facilitated a dialogue in South Africa, people began reflecting on apartheid in ways that surprised them. They were able to stand beside the tension of the topic without being identified with it. Similarly, in the healthcare dialogue, it was at this point that people began to discuss their status as "gods" and stopped blaming others in the "system" for the difficulties they saw.

As people participate, they also begin to watch the session in a new way. One participant from a group of urban leaders in Boston compared it to seeing the inside of their minds performing together in a theatre. People become sensitive to how habitual patterns of interaction can limit creative inquiry.

This phase can be playful and penetrating. Yet it also leads to crisis. People begin to feel the impact that fragmented ways of thinking has had on themselves, their organizations, and their culture. They sense their isolation. Such awareness brings pain—both from the loss of comforting beliefs and from exercising new cognitive and emotional muscles. The "crisis of collective pain" is the challenge of embracing these self-created limits of human experience. It is a deep and challenging crisis, one that requires considerable discipline and collective trust.

4. CREATIVITY IN THE CONTAINER

If the crisis of collective pain can be navigated, a new level of awareness opens. People begin to sense that they are participating in a pool of common meaning because they have sufficiently explored each other's views. They still may not agree, but their thinking takes on an entirely different rhythm and pace.

At this point, the distinction between memory and fresh thinking becomes apparent. People may find it hard to talk together using the rigid categories of previous understanding. The net of their thought is not fine enough to capture the subtle and delicate understandings that begin to emerge. People may find they do not have adequate words and fall silent. Yet the silence is not an empty void, but one replete with richness. Rumi, a 13th century Persian poet, captures this experience:

"Out beyond ideas of rightdoing and wrongdoing
There is a field
I will meet you there
When the soul lies down in that grass
The world is too full to talk about."

In this experience, the world is too full to talk *about*; too full to use language to analyze it. Yet words can also be evocative—narratives that convey richness of meaning. Though we may have few words for such experiences, dialogue raises the possibility of speech that clothes meaning, instead of words merely pointing towards it. I call this kind of experience metalogue, meaning "moving or flowing with."

Metalogue reveals a conscious, intimate, and subtle relationship between the structure and content of an exchange and its meaning. The medium and the message are linked: information from the process conveys as much meaning as the content of the words exchanged. The group does not "have" meaning, it *is* its meaning. Loosening rigid patterns of thought frees energy that now permits new levels of intelligence and creativity in the container.

Dialogue is not intended to be a problem-solving technique, but a means to explore the underlying incoherence of thought and action that gives rise to the problems we face. It balances more structured problem-solving approaches with the exploration of fundamental habits of attention and assumption behind traditional thinking. By providing a setting in which these subtle and tacit influences on our thinking can be altered, dialogue holds the potential for allowing entirely new kinds of collective intelligence to appear.

William Isaacs is the director of The Dialogue Project, which is a part of the Organizational Learning Center at MIT. He is currently conducting research on dialogue and organizational learning in corporate, political, and social settings around the world.

THE EMERGENCE OF LEARNING COMMUNITIES

by Stephanie Ryan

*"The union of Curiosity and Commitment
is barren without Experimentation.
They may dream of taking action,
but ideas are simply that, ideas.
Ideas are no substitute
for the life blood of exploration
found in Experimentation."*
　　　　　　　　—S. Ryan

Meeting the challenges that face our society today will require us to go beyond traditional organizational, gender, and ethnic boundaries. Learning in community offers one way to connect the fragmented thinking and acting that perpetuates continued suboptimization at the expense of the whole community.

Learning communities can be formed within or between "learning organizations" by redrawing boundaries to include the diversity of thought represented within each stakeholder group. The inclusion of diverse perspectives serves the whole community by broadening perspectives to frame the issue and helps to evaluate the effectiveness of actions. The sense of wholeness inherent in a learning community is captured in the African expression "it takes a whole village to educate a child."

A "community," in this sense, is a group of individuals who freely choose to be and do something together in an ongoing way (as opposed to typical teams within organizations, where the choice to participate can fade behind the everyday routine of going to the office and receiving a paycheck). A member of a learning community is rarely paid to show up; they are there out of their curiosity and commitment to create something that they care about. Learning community members are connected by matters of the heart as well as the mind.

Developing a learning community requires mastery of a collaborative learning process. A stunning example of a community that has both embraced and mastered collaboration is the Association of Mondragon Cooperatives in Spain. The Mondragon Cooperative was founded in 1956 with funds raised from local townspeople to open a small paraffin stove factory with 24 people. Today, they have over 160 cooperative enterprises, employing more than 23,000 members. Their actions are based on a single guiding principle: "How can we do this in a way that serves both those in the enterprise *and* those in the community equally, rather than serving one at the expense of the other?"[†]

For such collaboration to occur, a habit of thinking, acting, and communicating openly must emerge within the community. Creating a structure that can support this interaction is the first step to sustaining learning within the community. The "Collaborative Learning" diagram shows a reinforcing structure that can promote such learning, through joint experimentation that leads to reflection, shared insight, and improved collaborative design of future experimentation.

COLLABORATIVE DESIGN

Individual learning takes place, in part, through curiosity followed by experimentation. For collaborative learning to occur, *shared* curiosity needs to be present, which is translated into the choice of what to collectively explore. Members of the community need to make thoughtful and heartfelt choices about the journey of shared exploration they will embark on together.

Once the path has been chosen, designers who represent the whole

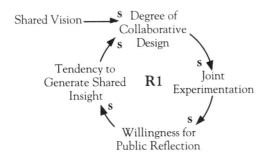

Shared Vision ——**s** Degree of
Collaborative
s Design

Tendency to
Generate Shared   **R1**   **s** Joint
Insight   Experimentation

s

s Willingness for
Public Reflection

For collaborative learning to occur, there must be shared design about what to explore. Experimenting together with a willingness to reflect collectively can lead to new shared insights, and therefore enhance future design.

system are selected. These designers—a diverse body of stakeholders with the potential for seeing things differently—cross many boundaries. The diversity inherent in these groups is essential to the design of a robust experiment.

JOINT EXPERIMENTATION

The designers are also the actors. Therefore, when collaborative design leads to joint experimentation, the experimenters know what they are looking for in terms of results and are genuinely curious about the outcome. Too often a set of people design an experiment and then ask some other set of people to go off and do it. This typically results in later questioning why the "implementation" failed and why the actors had no ownership in completing the "task."

PUBLIC REFLECTION

This continuity of design and experimentation creates the possibility for a common experience that can be publicly discussed afterward. The possibility of open reflection is only realized if the ability and willingness to share and suspend one's thoughts are also present. In my own work, I have found that the impact increases significantly when clients co-design interventions. After a meeting or offsite we speak candidly about what did and didn't work, without placing blame on the "consultant" for not knowing better or the "client" for being too closed-minded to appreciate an outside perspective. Out of our shared ownership, we create shared insight.

SHARED INSIGHT

If people can openly share their experiences, assumptions, and beliefs with one another about what they thought would happen (what the design was intended to produce) and what actually happened (the results of the joint experimentation), the discrepancy between the two can be perceived and hopefully understood. This process can yield shared insight into the nature of the issue and, if recorded in some form of group memory, can inform future collaborative designs.

Capturing a systemic "picture" of collaborative learning in a causal loop diagram illustrates the importance of the *process* of interaction rather than focusing on an individual player or an elusive end-state. Areas of highest leverage, where a small intervention can significantly affect the health of the system, can then be made more visible, understood, and implementable. The beauty of the circle is three-fold: you can start anywhere, it is never over, and there is no focus on individual blame (since everyone is responsible).

Causal loops can also help a learning community develop their on-going commitment to the collaborative journey of thinking, communicating and acting. The Mondragon Cooperative has drawn the circle defining "we" as the owner-employees, consumers, bank depositors, and the community. Hence it has not limited its activities to business and banking; rather it has participated in nearly every realm of community development, building over 40 cooperative housing complexes, creating private day care, grade school, high school, and higher education facilities.

LIMITS TO LEARNING

A systems thinker knows nothing grows forever. Consequently the question arises, "What are the limits to learning as a community?" These brakes to learning come in several forms: fear of failure, denial or perception of failure, or the inability to deal with diverse viewpoints gracefully. What all of these limits have in common is the net effect of increasing defensive behaviors in the community (fight or flight) at the expense of open reflection.

As we begin to learn together, our expectations of success start to grow (loop B2 in "Limits to Learning"). If expectations are growing, however, it becomes harder and harder for us to meet them. Fear of failure tends to emerge quickly. Although the group is successfully leaping impasses in its collective understanding, each new gap can seem farther apart than the last one, and uncertainty begins to grow.

LIMITS TO LEARNING

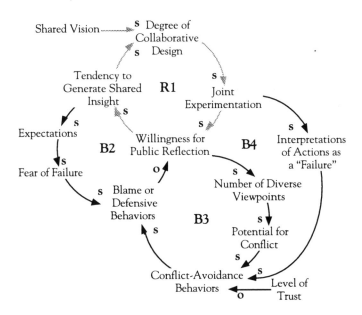

Limits to learning can come in several forms; as shared insight is generated, expectations heighten and a fear of failure can lead to defensive behaviors (B2). The diversity of viewpoints can also lead to conflict-avoidance behaviors, which can negatively affect the community's willingness to communicate openly (B3). Joint experimentation can also lead to interpreting actions as failures, rather than as opportunities for learning (B4).

When insecurity starts to increase, the need to be defended also grows. People enact defensive behaviors to avoid threat, embarrassment, conflict, and anything associated with being "wrong." Since "the best defense is a strong offense," people may even begin finger-pointing or blaming others as a means of escaping personal blame.

Defensive routines often appear in the form of denial, which quickly escalates from the personal to the collective (from *illusion* to *delusion* to *collusion*). At some level, I start telling myself, "Everything's fine, I hope." I begin to buy into this illusion and the need to believe everything is okay. If a community member and I collectively say that everything is okay (because we do not want to acknowledge any problems), we begin to delude ourselves about what is true. Consciously or unconsciously, we have collectively agreed not to question it. We collude not to inquire into the nature of our actions, and our performance becomes undiscussable. Unfortunately, our ability to reflect or collectively generate insights about the systems of which we are a part also deteriorates.

Yet another potential limit sprouts from the fertile ground of diverse stakeholders participating in the design phase. The greater the diversity of viewpoints, the higher the likelihood that people will interpret the different views as conflicting and shy away from exploring views and suspending assumptions. If conflict avoidance arises, open and honest reflection is undermined and the possibility of creating shared insight or learning dissipates (B3).

Another limit to learning results when an experiment is interpreted as a failure rather than another opportunity for learning. Once again, the need to avoid blame or justify money spent causes defensiveness to dominate over reflectiveness. Soon the collective learning breaks down as people begin to "posture" (sometimes politically) to look good. Information is no longer freely shared; in fact the willingness to look at the data is often undermined in the form of denial (B4).

The nature of the reinforcing loop (R1) is first virtuous, reflective and collective—"we're in this together." The balancing loops, however, represent distinctly protective, individualistic behavior—which is more about looking good, even at the expense of others (suboptimization). The virtuous circle becomes a vicious cycle. This is the land of the "hero," "lone ranger," or "rugged individualist" who can be counted on to pull it through in the end without needing help from anyone. Yet today's world of rapid change and complexity is making it harder and harder for any one hero to save the day, and the need for collaboration is painfully apparent.

What all these limits to learning in community have in common is the deterioration of relationships, whether it is a relationship with oneself or others. The "capacity constraint" in learning communities is the capacity for truth in relationship to oneself or others. This inability manifests itself as a barrier to honest communication.

EMPTINESS

In M. Scott Peck's book *The Different Drum*, his model of "community making" includes a stage that is not found in traditional team development models. He characterizes it as "emptiness." At the individual level, emptiness is about letting go of whatever is getting in the way of one's relationship to oneself or others. It may involve suspending assumptions, attributions, judgment, or expectations. In order for this to occur, however, we must first realize we have these assumptions (or mental models). Appreciating and understanding emptiness is crucial for managers who want to facilitate collaborative learning in their organizations (see "Stages of Community-Making").

A common dilemma managers face is "How can I facilitate collaborative learning if I can't do it myself—if I'm not even sure it's possible?" The temptation is to supply a ready-made solution. However, the real leverage lies in simply acknowledging that the dilemma is part of the journey; one of many that will be encountered along the path. To the extent this dilemma can be voiced, rather than hidden, it will enhance the community's learning. The moment it is denied, groups retreat into chaos or pseudo-community.

STAGES OF COMMUNITY-MAKING

Groups typically begin in pseudo-community, moving at their own pace through chaos and emptiness. Whether or not the group is able to reach community depends entirely on the dynamics and commitment of the group. There is significant overlap between the stages, and not everyone is in the same stage at the same time.

PSEUDO-COMMUNITY

• Members attempt to be loving and pleasant and inevitably fake it
• Expression of feelings is discouraged
• Disagreements and conflict are avoided, and individual differences are ignored
• Blanket statements and generalities prevail

CHAOS

• Individual differences surface
• Well-intended but misguided attempts to heal and convert
• People resist being changed, in turn try to convert the converters
• Members fight over whose beliefs are right, whose way will prevail
• Lack of direction, general feeling of struggle, going nowhere
• Attacks on leader for lack of structure; attempts to replace designated leader

EMPTINESS

• Bridge between chaos and community, where you suspend expectations and preconceptions
• Acknowledge fear of the unknown, able to admit "I don't know"
• Empty selves of prejudices, judgments based on little or no experience
• Discard any ideology, theology, and solution which assumes the status of "the one and only right way"

• Be present in service of whole; interpersonal differences appreciated and celebrated
• Increased capacity to surrender control, and acknowledge the possibility of failure
• Silent reflection on what needs to be emptied
• A kind of death necessary for rebirth; naked humanness is shared

COMMUNITY

• Inclusive, soft boundaries, no pressure to conform
• Full expression of the range of human emotions
• Commitment to co-exist, embracing and transcending differences
• Love, deep caring for self and others in relationship
• Humble and realistic in seeing our own and others' gifts and limitations
• Contemplative, willing and able to reflect on itself
• Unconditional acceptance which leads to healing
• No "sides," people can argue gracefully
• Total decentralization of authority, flow of leadership
• Spirit of peace; silence is welcomed

Source: M. Scott Peck. The Different Drum: Community Making and Peace. *New York: Touchstone—Simon & Schuster, Inc., 1987.*

LEADERSHIP IN LEARNING COMMUNITIES

Leadership in learning communities is shared; it moves freely as needed among the group members. This shared sense of responsibility is different from traditional teams, in which the leader is often held accountable by others if something isn't working as intended. In a learning community, however, each person feels equal responsibility for the "success" of the community's learning and is willing to look inwardly at what he or she is consciously or unconsciously doing to support or hinder the community's learning. The commitment to open and honest reflection is internally funded and renewed by the choice to be an ongoing member of the learning community.

I prefer to position the "leaders" of learning communities as facilitators or guides. Guides may make occasional comments on the journey, pointing out what is happening along the way, but they cannot lead a group into community—the group must choose for itself. What a guide can do is facilitate the emptying process by continually emptying him or herself and requesting the same of the group. Emptying in this case includes letting go of "old baggage" which may need to be discarded if it prevents members from truly listening or speaking with each other. For example, the most powerful thoughts and feelings I often need to empty are those of having to "fix" myself or others to make everything okay. Learning communities are thus born out of total acceptance of self and others—born out of trust.

LEARNING COMMUNITIES

On the other side of emptiness is community, and the only way over is "into and through." Emptiness is a time when the skills of dialogue are most needed (see "Dialogue: The Power of Collective Thinking," p. 83). The ability to dialogue can offer a bridge to the other side. I believe open communication begins with being willing and able to see, hear and feel myself. Silence is an invaluable intervention in this stage; quiet is needed to hear the soul speaking through us. When groups learn to dialogue together, meaning moves through the individuals—

learning occurs because individuals have emptied themselves and created room for perceiving and acting anew.

Peck's definition of community goes a long way to define what learning communities could mean: "A group of individuals who have learned to communicate honestly with each other, whose *relationships* go deeper than their masks of composure," and who have developed some significant commitment to "rejoice together, mourn together," and to "delight in each other, make others' conditions our own." To become masterful at these kinds of relationships is to build capacity for learning collaboratively, relieving the constraints of different limits to learning.

Peck goes further to state "there can be no vulnerability without risk; there can be no community without vulnerability; there can be no peace—and ultimately no life—without community." Nor can there be learning without vulnerability. If communities are a safe container for risk and vulnerability, then perhaps they will also be fertile ground for learning.

In many organizations I witness an oscillation between pseudo-community and chaos, where groups are caught in self-sealing vicious spirals. The undiscussable by its nature is undiscussable, which precludes open communication or relationships. If groups find themselves in emptiness, typically somebody (often a traditional leader) steps in to "fix" or make it better. Although the move is well-intended, it is counterproductive. Yet this is not apparent unless an appreciation for emptiness is present.

Emptiness is a healthy sign of development. Unfortunately, it is not yet part of a popular model of development and not often recognized by facilitators. Too often the traditional facilitator leads the retreat back to pseudo-community (pretending things are better than they are), or chaos (fixing people and converting them to a "right" point of view) because it is too difficult to be in a place of "not knowing."

Developing the capacity to live with emptiness means developing the capacity to be in relationship with oneself and others in learning communities. Cultivating emptiness offers a field to discuss the undiscussable and to make the invisible visible in a more reflective way. The experience of giving voice to what needs to be said, and seeing what has always been there, is the experience of learning in community.

Learning communities are places of truth-seeking and speaking without fear of reprisal or judgment. They are places where curiosity reigns over knowing and where experimentation is welcome. To develop the capacity to live with "not knowing"... to learn to be in relationship with oneself... to be reflective rather than defensive in nature... those are the challenges of learning to live in community.

[†]*"Mondragon: Archetype of Future Business?"* World Business Academy Perspectives, *1992, Vol. 6, No. 2, Berrett-Koehler Publishers.*

Stephanie Ryan, founder of In Care, is a facilitator of learning within communities. She regularly collaborates with clients in applying the disciplines of organizational learning. Stephanie welcomes others' stories and perspectives.

THE SPIRIT OF THE
LEARNING ORGANIZATION

by Daniel H. Kim and Eileen Mullen

At one point in the movie *Excalibur,* King Arthur lay weakened in bed as his whole kingdom crumbled around him. Most of his knights had already perished in the pursuit of the Holy Grail. But one knight, Perceval, was able to return with the secret of the Holy Grail—that the King and the land were one. The kingdom was decaying because King Arthur's spirit was dying. It was the bitterness in his own heart that had poisoned the land. The personal choice to let love and forgiveness into his own heart was what brought him and the kingdom back.

Merlin had foreshadowed Arthur's struggle when asked what was the most important thing in the world. "Truth," he answered. "That's the most important thing. When a man lies, he murders some part of the world."

When we live the truth, we are truly alive. *But when we live a lie, we kill everything around us.* Many people are beginning to acknowledge that the systemic problems and limitations we are currently experiencing—in our organizations, our government, the environment—are the result of our continuing to live a lie rather than face the truth of our connectedness.

We are awakening from a lie that we have been brought up to believe—that the individual is but a cog in the wheel of a great machine called industrial progress—to the realization that ours has been a misguided dream. The myth that human relationships could be broken down into their constituent parts, like the parts of a machine, is being replaced by a growing appreciation for the integrity of the whole and the realization that we are *all* interconnected with *everything*. If life is about a deep commitment to the truth, then the learning journey can be the awakening process.

COMMITMENT TO THE TRUTH

How many of us feel that commitment to the truth can comfortably extend to include our work environment? How much honesty can we afford? We have come to fear the truth—and truth-telling—in our organizations, especially when it differs from the "company line." We assume there must be a good reason for stifling the confrontations that would occur if everyone felt free to voice his or her own truth. We have a sense that chaos will take over—that order in our world will cease.

In a learning organization, the discipline of creating shared vision is rooted in personal mastery, and personal mastery is based on a commitment to the truth about current reality. That commitment provides us with a clear idea of where we are and what we believe and allows us to begin to build the creative tension that will propel us toward creating what we truly want (see "Creative Tension"). In order to generate creative tension, we need both a compelling vision and a clear understanding of our current reality. Without a

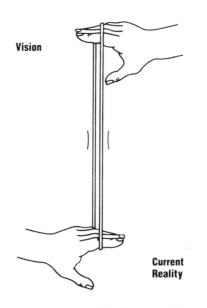

CREATIVE TENSION

Vision

Current
Reality

Source: *Sloan Management Review*

vision, there is no real motivation to change. Without a clear understanding of where we are, we have no basis for effective action.

Only if we can tell ourselves the truth about the current reality in our organizations can we open ourselves up to new possibilities for innovation and improvement. Only through a commitment to the truth can a learning organization articulate a meaningful set of values that can guide it on its journey (see "Values of a Learning Organization").

When we are unclear about our own truth, we muddy the environment around us. When we clearly express our own truth and also our shared truth—our values—we contribute to the constantly-generating field of energy we inhabit. In a "spirited" learning organization, the energy released with this kind of freedom is infectious. People like to come into this kind of space. When we do not have to censor what we really think and care about, we have more energy to devote to creating something that really matters to us.

MULTIPLE "TRUTHS"?

In this constantly-changing world, a universe that seems to thrive on diversity and multiplicity and complexity, we can no longer afford to focus our attention on one view or one group of people. Learning organizations need the energy of all of their members, as well as the vision, the aspirations, and the inspirations of everyone who is involved in them.

Peter Senge, author of *The Fifth Discipline*, emphasizes that ongoing conversations about personal visions are vital to creating an organization's shared vision. As important as building shared vision is, however, Senge notes that the hardest lesson for managers to accept is that "*there is nothing you can do to get another person to enroll or commit*" to a shared vision. "Enrollment and commitment require freedom of choice."

In the new documentary about Noam Chomsky called "Manufacturing Consent," the linguist challenges a young reporter who is condemning him for defending the rights of a professor in France who wrote a book claiming that the holocaust never happened. In reply, Chomsky said, "Free speech is not only for people you agree with. Stalin believed in that kind of free speech; Hitler believed in that kind of free speech. No, free speech is for those you don't agree with."

True democracy is based on a fundamental belief in the benefits of

VALUES OF A LEARNING ORGANIZATION

The spirit of a learning organization is created and sustained every day by the set of values that govern its actions. If the values are based on hierarchical, authoritarian, and punitive principles, the spirit of those who work under such conditions will reflect those values. A formal "Declaration of Values" may be needed to help bring out the creative and liberating spirit necessary for creating a learning organization. The following is proposed as a starting point:

As a learning organization...

We believe that each person deserves equal respect as a human being regardless of his or her role or job position.

We believe that each person should receive equal consideration in helping to develop to his or her full potential.

We believe that people's potential should be limited only by the extent of their aspirations, not the artificial barriers of organizational structures or other people's mental images.

We recognize that each person's view is valid and honor the life's experiences that shaped it.

We operate on the basis of openness and trust, to nurture an environment where truths can "unfold" and be heard.

We believe that no human being is more important than another, but each is important in a unique way.

We value people for who they are and not just for what (or who) they know.

     Reflections on Creating Learning Organizations

listening to as many varied, distinct, and disparate voices as can be heard. What holds people together is that belief in the freedom to speak, to disagree, to have a different view. When that freedom is absent, fragmentation, isolation, and hostility are the result.

"I wonder why we limit ourselves so quickly to one idea or one structure or one perception, or to the idea that 'truth' exists in objective form," questions Margaret Wheatley in her book *Leadership and the New Science*. "Why would we stay locked in our belief that there is one right way to do something, or one correct interpretation to a situation, when the universe welcomes diversity and seems to thrive on a multiplicity of meanings? Why would we avoid participation and worry only about its risks, when we need more and more eyes to evoke reality?"

Studies of chaos have pointed to how sensitive the universe is, and how important each individual piece is to the shape of the whole. This suggests that we need to encourage differences, rather than smooth them over. Wheatley states, "self-organizing systems demonstrate new relationships between autonomy and control, showing how a large system is able to maintain its overall form and identity only because it tolerates great degrees of individual freedom."

THE SUBSTANCE OF SPIRIT

Leadership and the New Science offers some interesting insights into the role of space in an organization. The book explores the more recent teachings of the "new science"—those discoveries in biology, chemistry, and physics that challenge us to reshape our world view. In particular, Margaret Wheatley's study of quantum physics, self-organizing systems, and chaos theory makes some challenging connections between our physical world and the organizations we create.

From quantum physics, we have discovered that we and our world are mostly space (99.999 percent of an atom is empty space). Wheatley suggests that this vast and invisible thing we call space is actually a *field*, teeming with information and resources, that we participate in whether we are aware of it or not.

"If we have not bothered to create a field of vision that is coherent and sincere, people will encounter other fields, the ones we have created unintentionally or casually," she explains. "As employees bump up against contradicting fields, their behavior mirrors those contradictions. We end up with what is common to many organizations, a jumble of behaviors and people going off in different directions, with no clear or identifiable pattern. What we lose when we fail to create consistent messages, when we fail to 'walk our talk,' is not just personal integrity. We lose the partnership of a field-rich space that can help bring form and order to the organization."

If space is not empty, but full of images and messages that we continually feed via our thoughts, words, and actions, then the content of our inner lives—our values, thoughts, and beliefs—has a powerful impact on the field of space, or spirit, within our organizations. *The quality of that field characterizes the spirit of an organization.* We create the field around us, whether it be one that inhibits individuals or encourages them to expand and participate. The field view of organizations suggests the importance of actively working to help shape the spirit of the learning organization.

LEADERSHIP

What is the role of the leader in creating this kind of space? The leader of an organization cannot be solely responsible for articulating the vision or spirit of an organization and disseminating it, because that spirit must come from the involvement of all individuals in the organization.

But leaders in learning organizations can help to foster these new ideas by "walking the talk," demonstrating by their own example that this is not a new flight of fancy, or the management solution-of-the-month. Leaders cannot force a tolerance of diversity; however, they can practice and encourage the exchange of views, especially ones that differ from their own.

We can let go of control as the predominant leadership style and choose to move in sync with the natural universe, which allows for more autonomy among its individual members. More importantly, we can choose to become conscious of our beliefs and attitudes and become more willing to see the effect they have on others in our organizations (see "Paradigm-Creating Loops: How Perceptions Shape Reality," p. 53).

Communication, explains Wheatley, is key to this task. "In the past, we may have thought of ourselves as skilled crafters of organizations, assembling the pieces of an organization, exerting our energy on the painstaking creation of links between all those parts. Now we need to imagine ourselves as broadcasters, tall radio beacons of information, pulsing out messages everywhere... Field creation is not just a task for senior managers. Every employee has energy to contribute; in a field-filled space, there are no unimportant players."

Systems thinking is a discipline that continually prods us to examine how our own actions create our reality and to identify ways in which we can change our own behavior to make a difference. With the help of new science discoveries and Margaret Wheatley's thoughts on their application to the way we view organizations, we have a new arena to explore—the unseen frontier of field-rich space.

Through exploring the values, truths, and meaning we find in the world, we can contribute to the generative spirit of a learning organization by bringing those intangibles to bear in our everyday lives, consciously and intentionally.

Our unique contribution toward building learning organizations may lie in our ability to know intimately the space we inhabit and how we contribute to the overall spirit of the enterprise. Perhaps that is the secret of the Holy Grail—to know the truth about ourselves, in whatever field we inhabit.

Further reading: Margaret Wheatley, Leadership and the New Science *(San Francisco: Berrett-Kohler, 1992), available through Pegasus Communications.*

Daniel H. Kim is the publisher of The Systems Thinker™ *and director of the Learning Lab Research Project at the MIT Organizational Learning Center.*
Eileen Mullen is a freelance writer living in Somerville, MA.

How Do You Know if Your Organization is Learning?

by Peter M. Senge

Since the publication of *The Fifth Discipline*, there has been a lot of activity and inquiry around the topic of how we can create learning organizations. One of the questions that many leaders ask is, "How do I know that learning is starting to occur in my organization as part of our daily activities?"

First of all, we shouldn't lose sight of the obvious: organizational learning has to do with improving performance. If a team is learning, we expect it to perform better. We wouldn't consider a basketball team that continues to perform below its potential—regardless of its intellectual sophistication—to be a learning team.

But gauging learning just by performance can be a trap. I think a common misconception these days is that organizational learning is synonymous with improving performance. People are saying, "if product development times, manufacturing cycle times, defect rates, etc. are getting better, then that organization is learning." But those figures can be misleading. A team or a company can do all the wrong things and get good performance for a short period of time. The employees may be taking short cuts that will kill them five years down the road in order to get those manufacturing cycle times down, or they can be improving one performance index by wreaking havoc in other parts of the organization. Likewise, a team or a company can be doing a lot of things right but the results won't show up for a while, either because of intrinsic delays or because there are forces outside their control that are depressing results.

Signs that organizational learning is occurring are a lot more subtle and harder to measure than performance indicators, primarily because we are not used to looking for them. The sort of things we are going to have to learn to look for are a feeling of spirit and energy throughout the organization, and a sense of alignment. We will have to learn how to recognize an insightful, internally-consistent diagnosis of a complex problem and a willingness among co-workers to continually test their favored diagnoses. People will start talking about their jobs differently. For example, you might ask someone "What are you doing?" and instead of rattling off their job description, they will refer to their sense of purpose, the customers they serve, and how their work interacts with others.

Another thing we would sense if an organization was learning is a difference in the quality of dialogue. There would be a real freedom among people to acknowledge what they don't know. An atmosphere of questioning and experimentation would exist at all levels of the organization. People would feel comfortable saying, "Here is where our thinking is right now and here is where we want to be," and would actively search out new ideas and input.

Perhaps surprisingly, there would also be a lot of conflict occurring in the organization. At Innovation Associates, we have often said that in highly-aligned groups there is much conflict of ideas. People's alignment—their commonality of purpose—gives them the confidence to disagree in a way they normally wouldn't. As people become partners in creating a common vision, they begin to feel a responsibility to challenge each other's thinking, in order to gain deeper levels of understanding needed to achieve that vision.

Along with this willingness to challenge thinking, an understanding of how to probe more effectively into other people's viewpoints is also required. Conflict then takes on a different meaning—it is no longer a personal attack, pitting one person's opinion against another.

Instead, it is a joint inquiry into how those differing perspectives can be combined to form a deeper understanding of the problem or issue at hand. This type of inquiry can show up in a conversation on the shop floor where one employee might say to another, "Oh, you don't see it the way I do? That's interesting. What leads you to see it differently?" We then start to see a greater balance between dialogues of inquiry and advocacy.

I think ultimately the truest sign of a learning organization at work will be when people begin to enter into these dialogues of joint inquiry instead of always advocating their positions. Then we can begin to learn what never could have been learned individually—no matter how bright we are, no matter how much time we take, and no matter how committed we are. What couldn't be learned individually will become possible as a group. *That* will be organizational learning.

Peter Senge, co-founder of Innovation Associates (Framingham, MA), is the director of the MIT Organizational Learning Center and author of The Fifth Discipline: The Art and Practice of the Learning Organization *(Doubleday, 1990).*

ABOUT THE AUTHORS

David Horne has been involved in the development of Human Dynamics since 1983.

William Isaacs is the director of The Dialogue Project, which is a part of the Organizational Learning Center at MIT. He is currently conducting research on dialogue and organizational learning in corporate, political, and social settings around the world.

Daniel H. Kim is the publisher of *The Systems Thinker*™ and director of the Learning Lab Research Project at the MIT Organizational Learning Center.

Fred Kofman is a professor at the MIT Sloan School of Management. He is directing one of the pilot projects of the MIT Organizational Learning Center, which explores ways to better coordinate the operations of a decentralized supply chain.

Eileen Mullen is a freelance writer living in Somerville, MA.

Robert Putnam is a partner in Action Design, a consulting firm based in Newton, MA. He is co-author with Chris Argyris and Diana McLain Smith of *Action Science* (Jossey-Bass, 1985).

Stephanie Ryan, founder of In Care, is a facilitator of learning within communities. She regularly collaborates with clients in applying the disciplines of organizational learning.

Sandra Seagal is founder and president of Human Dynamics International (Topanga, CA) and executive director of Human Dynamics Foundation. Both organizations are devoted to the development, empowerment, and sustainment of individual and collective human potential.

Peter Senge, co-founder of Innovation Associates (Framingham, MA), is the director of the MIT Organizational Learning Center and author of *The Fifth Discipline: The Art and Practice of the Learning Organization* (Double-day, 1990).

INDEX TO *THE SYSTEMS THINKER*™

PEGASUS

COMMUNICATIONS
I N C

Publishers of
The Systems Thinker™

Pegasus Communications, Inc.
PO Box 120 Kendall Square
Cambridge, MA 02142-0001

Pegasus Communications, Inc. is dedicated to helping organizations soar to new heights of excellence by helping managers explore, understand and articulate the challenges they face in managing the complexities of a changing business world. Its flagship publication, **The Systems Thinker™** newsletter, presents a systems perspective on current issues and provides "systems tools" for framing problems in new and insightful ways. Pegasus Communications also sponsors the annual **Systems Thinking in Action Conference**, where leading thinkers and practitioners from around the world meet to talk about the skills and capabilities of the learning organization. Pegasus' catalog, **The Learning Organization Resource Library**, offers videotapes and audiotapes from the conference, as well as books and other publications that explore the disciplines of the learning organization.

☐ Please send me more information regarding **Pegasus Communications'** resources and annual conference.

Name _____

Title _____

Company _____

Address _____

City _____ State _____ Zip _____

Country _____

Phone _____ Fax _____

Pegasus Communications, Inc.
PO Box 120 Kendall Square Cambridge, MA 02142-0001
Phone (617) 576-1231 • Fax (617) 576-3114